# Is There a
# Creator
# Who Cares About You?

D1533667

PUBLISHERS
WATCHTOWER BIBLE AND TRACT SOCIETY OF NEW YORK, INC.
INTERNATIONAL BIBLE STUDENTS ASSOCIATION
BROOKLYN, NEW YORK, U.S.A.


FIRST PRINTING IN ENGLISH:
5,000,000 COPIES

Photo Credits: **Cover:** J. Hester and P. Scowen (AZ State Univ.), NASA; **page 6:** Tompkins Collection/Courtesy of Museum of Fine Arts, Boston; **pages 12, 13, and 78:** Courtesy of Anglo-Australian Observatory, photographs by David Malin; **pages 14, 37, and 41:** UPI/Corbis-Bettmann; **page 22:** NASA photo; **page 76:** Acropolis, Athens; **page 86:** L. Ferrarese (Johns Hopkins University) and NASA; **page 89:** U.S. National Archives photo; **pages 91 and 117:** Culver Pictures; **page 107:** WHO photo by Edouard Boubat; **page 110:** Scroll: Courtesy of the Shrine of the Book, Israel Museum, Jerusalem; **page 115:** Courtesy of The British Museum; **pages 123, 129, and 136:** Pictorial Archive (Near Eastern History) Est.; **page 130:** Garo Nalbandian; **page 163:** Courtesy: Garden Tomb; **page 171:** From the book *Liberty's Victorious Conflict;* **page 179:** Rowboat: Garo Nalbandian

UNLESS OTHERWISE INDICATED,
SCRIPTURE QUOTATIONS ARE FROM THE MODERN-LANGUAGE
*NEW WORLD TRANSLATION OF THE HOLY SCRIPTURES—WITH REFERENCES*

*IS THERE A CREATOR WHO CARES ABOUT YOU?* ENGLISH (*ct*-E)
MADE IN THE UNITED STATES OF AMERICA

# CONTENTS

# CHAPTER ONE

# What Can Add Meaning to Your Life?

HAVE you dreamed of enjoying a better life, whether in your home area or in a tropical paradise? At one time or another, most of us have.

In 1891, French artist Paul Gauguin went to find such a life in French Polynesia. But reality soon set in. His dissolute past brought disease and suffering to himself and others. As he felt death approaching, he painted what has been described as a "final affirmation of artistic force." The book *Paul Gauguin 1848-1903—The Primitive Sophisticate* says: "The spectrum of human activity encompassed by the painting spans all of life, from birth to death . . . He was interpreting life as a great mystery."

Gauguin named that painting *"Where Do We Come From? What Are We? Where Are We Going?"*\*

Those questions may sound familiar. Many thinking people ask them. After noting man's scientific and technical advances, an editor of *The Wall Street Journal* wrote: "In the contemplation of man himself, of his dilemmas, of his place in this universe, we are little further along than when time began. We are still left with questions of who we are and why we are and where we are going."

True, some people are preoccupied with caring for their family, earning a living, traveling, or other personal interests because they know of no other

---

\* *D'où venons-nous? Que sommes-nous? Où allons-nous?*

*Gauguin's painting raised questions about the meaning of life*

meaning to life. Albert Einstein once said: "The man who regards his life as meaningless is not merely unhappy but hardly fit for life." In line with such thinking, some seek to put meaning in their life by pursuing the arts, scientific research, or humanitarian efforts to curb suffering. Do you know some like that?

It is understandable that basic questions about the meaning of life arise. How many parents after seeing a child die from malaria or another disease ask, Why such suffering? Is there meaning to it? Similar questions puzzle many young men and women who observe poverty, disease, and injustice. Brutal wars often lead people to wonder whether there can be meaning to life.

Even if you have not experienced such miseries, you might agree with Professor Freeman Dyson, who said: "I stand in good company when I ask again the questions [that the Biblical character] Job asked. Why do we suffer? Why is the world so unjust? What is the purpose of pain and tragedy?" You too might want the answers.

Finding satisfying answers would surely make a difference. A professor who endured the horrors of Auschwitz concentration camp observed: "There is nothing in the world . . . that would so effectively help one to survive even the worst conditions as the knowledge that there is a meaning in one's life." He felt that even one's mental health is linked to this search for meaning.

Over the centuries, many have sought answers through religion. After Gautama (Buddha) was exposed to the sight of a sick man, an old man, and a dead man, he sought enlightenment, or meaning, in religion but without belief in a personal God. Others have turned to their church.

What, though, about people today? Many focus on science, dismissing religion and "God" as irrelevant. "The more science progresses," comments *Religion and Atheism,* "the less room there seems to be for God. God has become a Displaced Person."

### Doing Without a Creator—Why?

Actually, the trend to dismiss religion or God has roots in philosophies of men who stressed pure reason. Charles Darwin felt that "natural selection" explains the living world better than does the existence of a Creator. Sigmund Freud taught that God was an illusion. And the view that 'God is dead' extends from the time of Friedrich Nietzsche down to our day. Oriental philosophies are similar. Teachers of Buddhism hold that there is no need to know about God. As to Shinto, Professor Tetsuo Yamaori stated that "gods are nothing but humans."

While skepticism about the existence of a Creator abounds, is it justified? Likely you know examples of 'scientific facts' that prevailed in the past but that in time were proved totally wrong. Views such as 'The earth is flat' and 'The whole universe revolves around our globe' prevailed for centuries, but we now know better.

What about later scientific ideas? For example, the 18th century philosopher David Hume—not accepting that there is a Creator—could offer no explanation for the complex biological design on earth. Darwin's theory proposed how life-forms developed, but it did not explain how life began or what meaning it has for us.

Consequently, many scientists as well as laymen sense that something is lacking. Scientific theories may try to explain *how?* but the key questions center on *why?* Even people raised amid belief in a Creator are affected. One young European history student said: "For me, God is dead. If he really did exist, there wouldn't be such a mess in the world: Innocent people are starving; animal species are going extinct . . . The idea of a Creator is nonsense." Given the conditions on earth, many cannot understand why a Creator—given that one exists—does not change things for the better.

Yet, we must admit that the reason many reject the existence of a Creator is that they do not *want* to believe. "Even if God were to tell me personally that I had to change my life," a European industrialist told an employee: "I still would not do it. I want to live my life the way I like it." Clearly, some feel that admitting the authority of a Creator would conflict with their freedom or with the life-style they prefer. They may proclaim, 'I only believe what I see, and I can't see any invisible Creator.'

Apart from *why* individuals have 'done without a Creator,' questions about life and its meaning persist. The day after man landed on the moon, theologian Karl Barth was asked about this technological triumph. He said: "It solves none of the problems that keep me awake at night." Today man is flying in space and speeding along in cyberspace. Still, thinking people see the need to have a purpose, something that gives meaning to their life.

We invite all who have an open mind to consider this subject. The book *Belief in God and Intellectual Honesty* notes that one who possesses "intellectual honesty" is characterized by a "readiness to scrutinize what one believes to be true" and "to pay sufficient attention to other evidence available."

In the subject at hand, such "evidence available" can help us to see whether there is a Creator behind life and the universe. And if a Creator exists, what might that One be like? Would a Creator have a personality that relates to our lives? Our considering this can shed light on how our lives can become more meaningful and rewarding.

# CHAPTER TWO

# How Did Our Universe Get Here? —The Controversy

ASTRONAUTS thrill to photograph the earth as it looms large through the window of a spacecraft. "That's the best part of flying in space," said one. But our earth seems very small when compared with the solar system. The sun could hold a million earths inside, with room to spare! However, could such facts about the universe have any bearing on your life and its meaning?

Let us take a brief mental trip into space to see our earth and sun in perspective. Our sun is just one of an awesome number of stars in a spiral arm of the Milky Way galaxy,* which itself is just a tiny part of the universe. With the naked eye, it is possible to see a few smudges of light that actually are other galaxies, such as the beautiful and larger Andromeda. The Milky Way, Andromeda, and some 20 other galaxies are bound gravitationally into a cluster, all of these being only a small neighborhood in a vast supercluster. The universe contains countless superclusters, and the picture does not end there.

The clusters are not evenly distributed in space. On a grand scale, they look like thin sheets and filaments around vast bubblelike voids. Some features are so long and wide that they resemble great walls.

---

* The Milky Way galaxy is some 600 quadrillion miles in diameter—yes, 600,000,000,000,000,000 miles! It takes light 100,000 *years* to cross it, and this one galaxy contains over 100 billion stars!

This may surprise many who think that our universe created itself in a chance cosmic explosion. "The more clearly we can see the universe in all its glorious detail," concludes a senior writer for *Scientific American,* "the more difficult it will be for us to explain with a simple theory how it came to be that way."

## Evidence Pointing to a Beginning

All the individual stars you see are in the Milky Way galaxy. Until the 1920's, that seemed to be the only galaxy. You probably know, though, that observations with larger telescopes have since proved otherwise. Our universe contains at least 50,000,-000,000 galaxies. We do not mean 50 billion *stars* —but at least 50 billion *galaxies,* each with billions of stars like our sun. Yet it was not the staggering quantity of huge galaxies that shook scientific beliefs in the 1920's. It was that they are all in motion.

Astronomers discovered a remarkable fact: When galactic light was passed through a prism, the light waves were seen to be stretched, indicating motion away from us at great speed. The more distant a galaxy, the faster it appeared to be receding. That points to an expanding universe!*

---

* In 1995, scientists noticed the strange behavior of the most distant star (SN 1995K) ever observed as it exploded in its galaxy. Like supernovas in nearby galaxies, this star became very bright and then slowly faded but over a longer period than ever before detected. *New Scientist* magazine plotted this on a graph and explained: "The shape of the light curve . . . is stretched in time by exactly the amount expected if the galaxy was receding from us at nearly half the speed of light." The conclusion? This is "the best evidence yet that the Universe really is expanding."

Even if we are neither professional astronomers nor amateurs, we can see that an expanding universe would have profound implications about our past—and perhaps our personal future too. Something must have started the process—a force powerful enough to overcome the immense gravity of the entire universe. You have good reason to ask, 'What could be the source of such dynamic energy?'

Although most scientists trace the universe back

*Our sun (box) is insignificant in the Milky Way galaxy, as illustrated here with spiral galaxy NGC 5236*

to a very small, dense beginning (a singularity), we cannot avoid this key issue: "If at some point in the past, the Universe was once close to a singular state of infinitely small size and infinite density, we have to ask what was there before and what was outside the Universe. . . . We have to face the problem of a Beginning."—Sir Bernard Lovell.

This implies more than just a source of vast energy. Foresight and intelligence are also needed

*The Milky Way contains over 100 billion stars, and it is only one of over 50 billion galaxies in the known universe*

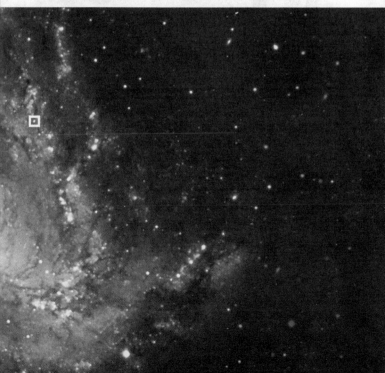

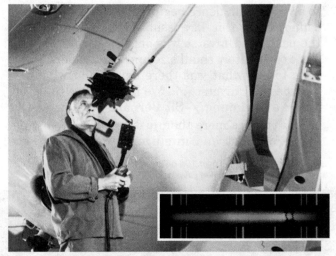

*Astronomer Edwin Hubble (1889-1953) realized that a red shift in light from distant galaxies showed that our universe is expanding and thus had a beginning*

because the rate of expansion seems very finely tuned. "If the Universe had expanded one million millionth part faster," said Lovell, "then all the material in the Universe would have dispersed by now. . . . And if it had been a million millionth part slower, then gravitational forces would have caused the Universe to collapse within the first thousand million years or so of its existence. Again, there would have been no long-lived stars and no life."

## Attempts to Explain the Beginning

Can experts now explain the origin of the universe? Many scientists, uncomfortable with the idea that the universe was created by a higher intelligence, speculate that by some mechanism it created itself out of nothing. Does that sound reasonable to you? Such speculations usually involve some variation of a theory (inflationary universe model)* conceived in 1979 by physicist Alan Guth. Yet, more recently, Dr. Guth admitted that his theory "does

---

* The inflation theory speculates as to what happened a fraction of a second after the beginning of the universe. Advocates of inflation hold that the universe was initially submicroscopic and then inflated faster than the speed of light, a claim that cannot be tested in a laboratory. Inflation remains a debated theory.

---

### Trying to Number the Stars

It is estimated that the Milky Way galaxy has more than 100,000,000,000 (100 billion) stars. Picture an encyclopedia devoting one page to each of these stars —our sun and the rest of our solar system would be limited to one page. How many volumes would the set need to have in order to cover the stars in the Milky Way?

With volumes of reasonable thickness, it is said that the encyclopedia would not fit in the New York Public Library, with its 256 miles of shelf space!

How long would it take you to examine those pages? "To flip through it, at the rate of a page per second, would require over ten thousand years," explains *Coming of Age in the Milky Way.* Yet the stars making up our galaxy are but a small fraction of the stars in the estimated 50,000,000,000 (50 billion) galaxies in the universe. If the encyclopedia contained a page for each of these stars, it would not fit on all the library shelves on earth. "The more we know about the universe," notes the book, "the more we come to see how little we know."

---

### Jastrow—On the Beginning

Robert Jastrow, Professor of Astronomy and Geology at Columbia University, wrote: "Few astronomers could have anticipated that this event—the sudden birth of the Universe—would become a proven scientific fact, but observations of the heavens through telescopes have forced them to that conclusion."

He then commented on the implications: "The astronomical proof of a Beginning places scientists in an awkward position, for they believe that every effect has a natural cause . . . The British astronomer E. A. Milne wrote, 'We can make no propositions about the state of affairs [in the beginning]; in the Divine act of creation God is unobserved and unwitnessed.' "—*The Enchanted Loom—Mind in the Universe.*

---

not explain how the universe arose from nothing." Dr. Andrei Linde was more explicit in a *Scientific American* article: "Explaining this initial singularity—where and when it all began—still remains the most intractable problem of modern cosmology."

If experts cannot really explain either the origin or the early development of our universe, should we not look elsewhere for an explanation? Indeed, you have valid reasons to consider some evidence that many have overlooked but that may give you real insight on this issue. The evidence includes the precise measurements of four fundamental forces that are responsible for all properties and changes affecting matter. At the mere mention of fundamental forces, some may hesitate, thinking, 'That's solely for physicists.' Not so. The basic facts are worth considering because they affect us.

## Fine-Tuning

The four fundamental forces come into play both in the vastness of the cosmos and in the infinite smallness of atomic structures. Yes, everything we see around us is involved.

Elements vital for our life (particularly carbon, oxygen, and iron) could not exist were it not for the fine-tuning of the four forces evident in the universe. We already mentioned one force, *gravity*. Another is the *electromagnetic force*. If it were significantly weaker, electrons would not be held around the nucleus of an atom. 'Would that be serious?' some might wonder. Yes, because atoms could not combine to form molecules. Conversely, if this force were much stronger, electrons would be trapped on the nucleus of an atom. There could be no chemical reactions between atoms—meaning no life. Even from this standpoint, it is clear that our existence and life depend on the fine-tuning of the electromagnetic force.

---

### Four Fundamental Physical Forces

1. Gravity—a very weak force on the level of atoms. It affects large objects—planets, stars, galaxies.

2. Electromagnetism—the key attracting force between protons and electrons, allowing molecules to form. Lightning is one evidence of its power.

3. Strong nuclear force—the force that glues protons and neutrons together in the nucleus of an atom.

4. Weak nuclear force—the force that governs the decay of radioactive elements and the efficient thermonuclear activity of the sun.

And consider the cosmic scale: A slight difference in the electromagnetic force would affect the sun and thus alter the light reaching the earth, making photosynthesis in plants difficult or impossible. It could also rob water of its unique properties, which are vital for life. So again, the precise tuning of the electromagnetic force determines whether we live or not.

Equally vital is the intensity of the electromagnetic force in relation to the other three. For example, some physicists figure this force to be 10,000,-000,000,000,000,000,000,000,000,000,000,000,000 ($10^{40}$) *times* that of gravity. It might seem a small change to that number to add one more zero ($10^{41}$). Yet that would mean that gravity is proportionally *weaker,* and Dr. Reinhard Breuer comments on the resulting situation: "With lower gravity the stars would be smaller, and the pressure of gravity in their interiors would not drive the temperature high enough for nuclear fusion reactions to get under way: the sun would be unable to shine." You can imagine what that would mean for us!

What if gravity were *stronger* proportionately, so that the number had only 39 zeros ($10^{39}$)? "With just this tiny adjustment," continues Breuer, "a star like the sun would find its life expectancy sharply reduced." And other scientists consider the fine-tuning to be even more precise.

Indeed, two remarkable qualities of our sun and other stars are long-term efficiency and stability. Consider a simple illustration. We know that to run efficiently, an automobile engine needs a critical ratio between fuel and air; engineers design complex

*Fine-tuning of forces that control our sun results in conditions just right for our life on earth*

mechanical and computer systems to optimize performance. If that is so with a mere engine, what of the efficiently "burning" stars such as our sun? The key forces involved are precisely tuned, optimized for life. Did that precision just happen? The ancient man Job was asked: "Did you proclaim the rules that govern the heavens, or determine the laws of nature on earth?" (Job 38:33, *The New English Bible*) No human did. So from where does the precision come?

## The Two Nuclear Forces

The structure of the universe involves much more than fine-tuning just gravity and the electromagnetic force. Two other physical forces also relate to our life.

These two forces operate in the nucleus of an atom, and they give ample evidence of forethought. Consider the *strong nuclear force,* which glues protons and neutrons together in the nucleus of the atom. Because of this bonding, various elements can form—light ones (such as helium and oxygen) and heavy ones (such as gold and lead). It seems that if this binding force were a mere 2-percent weaker, only hydrogen would exist. Conversely, if this force were slightly stronger, only heavier elements, but no hydrogen, could be found. Would our lives be affected? Well, if the universe lacked hydrogen, our sun would not have the fuel it needs to radiate life-giving energy. And, of course, we would have no water or food, since hydrogen is an essential ingredient of both.

---

### "Combination of Coincidences"

"Make the weak force slightly stronger and no helium would have been produced; make it slightly weaker and nearly all the hydrogen would have been converted into helium."

"The window of opportunity for a universe in which there is some helium and there are also exploding supernovas is very narrow. Our existence depends on this combination of coincidences, and on the even more dramatic coincidence of nuclear energy levels predicted by [astronomer Fred] Hoyle. Unlike all previous generations, we know how we come to be here. But, like all previous generations, we still do not know why." —*New Scientist.*

The fourth force in this discussion, called the *weak nuclear force,* controls radioactive decay. It also affects thermonuclear activity in our sun. 'Is this force fine-tuned?' you might ask. Mathematician and physicist Freeman Dyson explains: "The weak [force] is millions of times weaker than the nuclear force. It is just weak enough so that the hydrogen in the sun burns at a slow and steady rate. If the weak [force] were much stronger or much weaker, any forms of life dependent on sunlike stars would again be in difficulties." Yes, this precise rate of burning keeps our earth warm—but not incinerated—and keeps us alive.

Furthermore, scientists believe that the weak force plays a role in supernova explosions, which they give as the mechanism for producing and distributing most elements. "If those nuclear forces were in any way slightly different from the way they actually are, the stars would be incapable of making the elements of which you and I are composed," explains physicist John Polkinghorne.

More could be said, but you likely understand the point. There is an amazing degree of fine-tuning in these four fundamental forces. "All around us, we seem to see evidence that nature got it just right," wrote Professor Paul Davies. Yes, the precise tuning of the fundamental forces has made possible the existence and operation of our sun, our delightful planet with its life-sustaining water, our atmosphere so vital for life, and a vast array of precious chemical elements on earth. But ask yourself, 'Why such precise tuning, and from where?'

**Earth's Ideal Features**

Our existence requires precision in other respects as well. Consider the earth's measurements and its position relative to the rest of our solar system. The Bible book of Job contains these humbling questions: "Where did you happen to be when I founded the earth? . . . Who set its measurements, in case you know?" (Job 38:4, 5) As never before, those questions beg for answers. Why? Because of the amazing things that have been discovered about our earth—including its size and its position in our solar system.

No planet like earth has been found elsewhere in the universe. True, some scientists point to indirect evidence that certain stars have orbiting them objects that are hundreds of times larger than the earth. Our earth, though, is just the right size for our existence. In what sense? If earth were slightly larger, its gravity would be stronger and hydrogen, a light gas, would collect, being unable to escape the earth's gravity. Thus, the atmosphere would be inhospitable to life. On the other hand, if our earth were slightly smaller, life-sustaining oxygen would

"The special conditions on earth resulting from its ideal size, element composition, and nearly circular orbit at a perfect distance from a long-lived star, the sun, made possible the accumulation of water on the earth's surface." (*Integrated Principles of Zoology*, 7th edition) Life on earth could not have appeared without water.

escape and surface water would evaporate. In either case, we could not live.

The earth is also at an ideal distance from the sun, a factor vital for life to thrive. Astronomer John Barrow and mathematician Frank Tipler studied "the ratio of the Earth's radius and distance from the Sun." They concluded that human life would not exist "were this ratio slightly different from what it is observed to be." Professor David L. Block notes: "Calculations show that had the earth been situated only 5 per cent closer to the sun, a runaway greenhouse effect [overheating of the earth] would have occurred about 4 000 million years ago. If, on the other hand, the earth were placed only 1 per cent further from the sun, runaway glaciation [huge sheets of ice covering much of the globe] would have occurred some 2 000 million years ago."—*Our Universe: Accident or Design?*

To the above precision, you can add the fact that the earth rotates on its axis once a day, the right speed to produce moderate temperatures. Venus takes 243 days to rotate. Just think if the earth took as long! We could not survive the extreme temperatures resulting from such long days and nights.

Another vital detail is our earth's path around the sun. Comets have a wide elliptic path. Thankfully, this is not so with the earth. Its orbit is almost circular. Again, this prevents us from experiencing death-dealing extremes of temperature.

Nor should we ignore the location of our solar system. Were it nearer the center of the Milky Way galaxy, the gravitational effect of neighboring stars would distort the orbit of the earth. In contrast,

---

### Believe Only What You See?

Many rational people accept the existence of things they cannot see. In January 1997, *Discover* magazine reported that astronomers detected what they concluded were about a dozen planets orbiting distant stars.

"So far the new planets are known only from the way their gravity perturbs the motion of the parent stars." Yes, for the astronomers, the visible effects of gravity constituted a basis for believing in the existence of unseen heavenly bodies.

Related evidence—not direct observation—was an adequate basis for scientists to accept what was yet invisible. Many who believe in a Creator conclude that they have a similar basis for accepting what they cannot see.

---

were it situated at the very edge of our galaxy, the night sky would be all but devoid of stars. Starlight is not essential to life, but does it not add great beauty to our night sky? And based on current concepts of the universe, scientists have calculated that at the edges of the Milky Way, there would not have been enough of the needed chemical elements to form a solar system like ours.*

### Law and Order

From personal experience, you likely know that all things tend toward disorder. As any homeowner has observed, when left to themselves, things tend to break down or disintegrate. Scientists re-

---

* Scientists have found that the elements reveal amazing order and harmony. Interesting evidence is presented in the Appendix "Architectural Units of the Universe," page 26.

fer to this tendency as "the second law of thermodynamics." We can see this law at work daily. If left alone, a new automobile or bicycle will become scrap. Abandon a building and it will become a ruin. What about the universe? The law applies there too. So you might think that the order throughout the universe should give way to complete disorder.

However, this does not seem to be happening to the universe, as Professor of Mathematics Roger Penrose discovered when he studied the state of disorderliness (or, entropy) of the observable universe. A logical way to interpret such findings is to conclude that the universe started off in an ordered state and is still highly organized. Astrophysicist Alan Lightman noted that scientists "find it mysterious that the universe was created in such a highly ordered condition." He added that "any successful theory of cosmology should ultimately explain this entropy problem"—why the universe has not become chaotic.

In fact, our existence is contrary to this recognized law. So why is it that we are alive here on earth? As previously noted, that is a basic question that we should want answered.

---

Sir Fred Hoyle explains in *The Nature of the Universe*: "To avoid the issue of creation it would be necessary for all the material of the Universe to be infinitely old, and this it cannot be. . . . Hydrogen is being steadily converted into helium and the other elements . . . How comes it then that the Universe consists almost entirely of hydrogen? If matter were infinitely old this would be quite impossible. So we see that the Universe being what it is, the creation issue simply cannot be dodged."

# APPENDIX

## "Architectural Units of the Universe"

That is how a modern encyclopedia of science describes the chemical elements. There is amazing variety among the elements of our earth; some of them are rare; others are abundant. Elements such as gold may attract the human eye. Others are gases that we do not even see, such as nitrogen and oxygen. Each element is made of a certain kind of atom. How the atoms are constructed and relate to one another bespeaks economy and awesome organization in chartlike order.

About 300 years ago, only 12 elements were known—antimony, arsenic, bismuth, carbon, copper, gold, iron, lead, mercury, silver, sulfur, and tin. As more were discovered, scientists noticed that the elements reflected a distinct order. Because there were gaps in the order, scientists such as Mendeleyev, Ramsay, Moseley, and Bohr theorized the existence of unknown elements and their characteristics. Those elements were subsequently discovered just as predicted. Why could those scientists predict that there were forms of matter that were unknown at the time?

Well, the elements follow a natural numerical order based on the structure of their atoms. This is a proven law. Thus, school textbooks can set out a periodic table of elements in rows and columns —hydrogen, helium, and so on.

The *McGraw-Hill Encyclopedia of Science & Technology* observes: "Few systemizations in the history of science can rival the periodic concept as a broad revelation of the order of the physical world. . . . Whatever new elements may be discovered in the future, it is certain they will find a place in the periodic system, conforming to its order and exhibiting the proper familial characteristics."

When the elements are arranged in the rows and columns of the periodic table, a remarkable relationship is seen between elements that share a column. For example, in the last column are located helium (No. 2), neon (No. 10), argon (No. 18), krypton (No. 36), xenon (No. 54), and radon (No. 86). These are gases that glow brightly when an electric discharge passes through them, and they are used in some light bulbs. Also, they do not react easily with various elements, as do some other gases.

Yes, the universe—even down to its atomic particles—reveals astonishing harmony and order. What is responsible for such order, harmony, and variety among the building blocks of the universe?

# Periodic Table of the Elements

| | | | | | | | | | | | | | | | | | RARE GASES VIII |
|---|---|---|---|---|---|---|---|---|---|---|---|---|---|---|---|---|---|

helium He 2

| I | II | | | | | | | | | | | | III | IV | V | VI | VII | |
|---|---|---|---|---|---|---|---|---|---|---|---|---|---|---|---|---|---|---|

NONMETALS

METALS

TRANSITION ELEMENTS

hydrogen — Name of element
H — Symbol
1 — Atomic number

lithium Li 3 | beryllium Be 4

boron B 5 | carbon C 6 | nitrogen N 7 | oxygen O 8 | fluorine F 9 | neon Ne 10

sodium Na 11 | magnesium Mg 12

aluminum Al 13 | silicon Si 14 | phosphorus P 15 | sulfur S 16 | chlorine Cl 17 | argon Ar 18

potassium K 19 | calcium Ca 20 | scandium Sc 21 | titanium Ti 22 | vanadium V 23 | chromium Cr 24 | manganese Mn 25 | iron Fe 26 | cobalt Co 27 | nickel Ni 28 | copper Cu 29 | zinc Zn 30 | gallium Ga 31 | germanium Ge 32 | arsenic As 33 | selenium Se 34 | bromine Br 35 | krypton Kr 36

rubidium Rb 37 | strontium Sr 38 | yttrium Y 39 | zirconium Zr 40 | niobium Nb 41 | molybdenum Mo 42 | technetium Tc 43 | ruthenium Ru 44 | rhodium Rh 45 | palladium Pd 46 | silver Ag 47 | cadmium Cd 48 | indium In 49 | tin Sn 50 | antimony Sb 51 | tellurium Te 52 | iodine I 53 | xenon Xe 54

cesium Cs 55 | barium Ba 56 | lanthanum La 57 | hafnium Hf 72 | tantalum Ta 73 | tungsten W 74 | rhenium Re 75 | osmium Os 76 | iridium Ir 77 | platinum Pt 78 | gold Au 79 | mercury Hg 80 | thallium Tl 81 | lead Pb 82 | bismuth Bi 83 | polonium Po 84 | astatine At 85 | radon Rn 86

francium Fr 87 | radium Ra 88 | actinium Ac 89 | 104 | 105 | 106 | 107 | 108 | 109

Lanthanide series | cerium Ce 58 | praseodymium Pr 59 | neodymium Nd 60 | promethium Pm 61 | samarium Sm 62 | europium Eu 63 | gadolinium Gd 64 | terbium Tb 65 | dysprosium Dy 66 | holmium Ho 67 | erbium Er 68 | thulium Tm 69 | ytterbium Yb 70 | lutetium Lu 71

Actinide series | thorium Th 90 | protactinium Pa 91 | uranium U 92 | neptunium Np 93 | plutonium Pu 94 | americium Am 95 | curium Cm 96 | berkelium Bk 97 | californium Cf 98 | einsteinium Es 99 | fermium Fm 100 | mendelevium Md 101 | nobelium No 102 | lawrencium Lr 103

*Do the order and harmony of elements in the periodic table reflect mere chance or intelligent design?*

# CHAPTER THREE

# What Is the Origin of Life?

OUR earth teems with life. From the snowy Arctic to the Amazon rain forest, from the Sahara Desert to the Everglades swamp, from the dark ocean floor to bright mountain peaks—life abounds. And it is loaded with the potential to amaze us.

It comes in types, sizes, and quantities that stagger the imagination. A million species of insects hum and wiggle on our planet. In the waters around us swim over 20,000 species of fish —some the size of a grain of rice, others as long as a truck. At least 350,000 plant species—some weird, most wonderful—embellish the land. And over 9,000 species of birds fly overhead. These creatures, including man, form the panorama and symphony that we refer to as life.

But more amazing than the delightful variety around us is the profound unity linking them. Biochemists, who peek beneath the skin of earth's creatures, explain that all living things—be they amoebas or humans—depend on an awesome interaction: the teamwork between nucleic acids (DNA and RNA) and protein molecules. The intricate processes involving these components occur in virtually all our body cells, as it does in the cells of hummingbirds, lions, and whales. This uniform interaction produces a beautiful mosaic of life. How did this orchestration of life come about? In fact, what is the origin of life?

Likely you accept that at one time the earth had no life on it. Scientific opinion agrees, and so do many religious books. Still, you may realize that those two sources—science and religion—differ in explaining how life began on earth.

Millions of people of all educational levels believe that an intelligent Creator, the original Designer, produced life on earth. In contrast, many

## How Much Chance for Chance?

"Chance, and chance alone, did it all, from the primeval soup to man," said Nobel laureate Christian de Duve, speaking about the origin of life. Is chance, though, a rational explanation for the cause of life?

What is chance? Some think in terms of a mathematical probability, such as the chance involved in flipping a coin. However, that is not how many scientists use "chance" regarding the origin of life. The vague word "chance" is used as a substitute for a more precise word such as "cause," especially when the cause is not known.

"To personify 'chance' as if we were talking about a causal agent," notes biophysicist Donald M. MacKay, "is to make an illegitimate switch from a *scientific* to a quasi-religious *mythological* concept." Similarly, Robert C. Sproul points out: "By calling the unknown cause 'chance' for so long, people begin to forget that a substitution was made. . . . The assumption that 'chance equals an unknown cause' has come to mean for many that 'chance equals cause.'"

Nobel laureate Jacques L. Monod, for one, used this chance-equals-cause line of reasoning. "Pure chance, absolutely free but blind, [is] at the very root of the stupendous edifice of evolution," he wrote. "Man knows at last that he is alone in the universe's unfeeling immensity, out of which he emerged only by chance." Note he says: 'BY chance.' Monod does what many others do —he elevates chance to a creative principle. Chance is offered as the means by which life came to be on earth.

In fact, dictionaries show that "chance" is "the assumed impersonal purposeless determiner of unaccountable happenings." Thus, if one speaks about life coming about by chance, he is saying that it came about by a causal power that is not known. Could it be that some are virtually spelling "Chance" with a capital letter —in effect saying, Creator?

scientists say that life arose from nonliving matter, one chemical step after another, merely by chance. Is it one, or is it the other?

We should not think that this issue is rather remote from us and from our finding a more meaningful life. As already noted, one of the very fundamental questions humans have sought to answer is, Where did we as living humans come from?

Most science courses focus on the adaptation and survival of life-forms instead of on the more central question of the very origin of life. You may have noted that attempts to explain where life came from are usually presented in generalizations such as: 'Over millions of years, molecules in collision somehow produced life.' Yet, is that really satisfying? It would mean that in the presence of energy from the sun, lightning, or volcanoes, some lifeless matter moved, became organized, and eventually started living—all of this without directed assistance. What a huge leap that would have been! From nonliving matter to living! Could it have occurred that way?

Back in the Middle Ages, accepting such a concept might not have seemed a problem because spontaneous generation—the notion that life could arise spontaneously from nonliving matter—was a prevailing belief. Finally, in the 17th century, Italian physician Francesco Redi proved that maggots appeared in rotten meat only after flies had laid eggs on it. No maggots developed on meat that flies could not reach. If animals as big as flies did not just appear on their own, what about the microbes that kept appearing in food—covered or not? Although later experiments indicated that microbes did not arise spontaneously, the issue remained controversial. Then came the work of Louis Pasteur.

Many people recall Pasteur's work in solving problems related to fermentation and to infectious disease. He also performed experiments to determine whether tiny life-forms could arise by themselves. As you may have read, Pasteur demonstrated that even minute bacteria did not form in sterilized water protected from contamination. In 1864 he announced: "Never will the doctrine of spontaneous generation recover from the mortal blow struck by this simple experiment." That statement remains true. No experiment has ever produced life from nonliving matter.

How then could life come to be on earth? Modern efforts to answer that question might be dated to the 1920's, to the work of Russian biochemist Alexander I. Oparin. He and other scientists since then have offered something like the script of a three-act drama that depicts what is claimed to have occurred on the stage of planet Earth. The first act portrays earth's elements, or raw materials, being transformed into groups of molecules. Then comes the jump to large molecules. And the last act of this drama presents the leap to the first living cell. But did it really happen that way?

Fundamental to that drama is explaining that earth's early atmosphere was much different from what it is today. One theory assumes that free oxygen was virtually absent and that the elements nitrogen, hydrogen, and carbon formed ammonia

*Many scientists now acknowledge that the complex molecules basic to life could not have been spontaneously generated in some prebiotic soup*

and methane. The concept is that when lightning and ultraviolet light struck an atmosphere of these gases and water vapor, sugars and amino acids developed. Bear in mind, though, that this is theory.

According to this theoretical drama, such molecular forms washed into the oceans or other bodies of water. Over time, sugars, acids, and other compounds concentrated into a broth of "prebiotic soup" where amino acids, for instance, joined to become proteins. Extending this theoretical progression, other compounds called nucleotides formed chains and became a nucleic acid, such as DNA. All of this supposedly set the stage for the final act of the molecular drama.

One might depict this last act, *which is undocumented,* as a love story. Protein molecules and DNA molecules happen to meet, recognize each other, and embrace. Then, just before the curtain rings down, the first living cell is born. If you were following this drama, you might wonder, 'Is this real life or fiction? Could life on earth really have originated in this way?'

### Genesis in the Laboratory?

In the early 1950's, scientists set out to test Alexander Oparin's theory. It was an established fact that life comes *only* from life, yet scientists theorized that if conditions differed in the past, life might have come *slowly* from nonlife. Could that be demonstrated? Scientist Stanley L. Miller, working in the laboratory of Harold Urey, took hydrogen, ammonia, methane, and water vapor (assuming that this had been the primitive atmosphere), sealed these in a flask with boiling water at the bottom (to represent an ocean), and zapped electric sparks (like lightning) through the vapors. Within a week, there were traces of reddish goo, which Miller analyzed and found to be rich in amino acids —the essence of proteins. You may well have heard of this experiment because for years it has been cited in science textbooks and school courses as if it explains how life on earth began. But does it?

Actually, the value of Miller's experiment is seriously questioned today. (See "Classic but Questionable," pages 36-7.) Nevertheless, its apparent success led to other tests that even produced components found in nucleic acids (DNA or RNA). Specialists in the field (sometimes called origin-of-life scientists) felt optimistic, for they had seemingly replicated the first act of the molecular drama. And it seemed as though laboratory versions of the remaining two acts would follow. One chemistry professor claimed: "The explanation of the origin of a primitive living system by evolutionary mechanisms is well within sight." And a science writer observed: "Pundits speculated that scientists, like Mary Shelley's Dr. Frankenstein, would shortly conjure up living organisms in their laboratories and thereby demonstrate in detail how genesis unfolded." The mystery of the spontaneous origin of life, many thought, was solved.—See "Right Hand, Left Hand," page 38.

## Moods Change—Riddles Remain

In the years since, however, that optimism has evaporated. Decades have passed, and life's secrets remain elusive. Some 40 years after his experiment, Professor Miller told *Scientific American:* "The problem of the origin of life has turned out to

---

"[The smallest bacterium] is so much more like people than Stanley Miller's mixtures of chemicals, because it already has these system properties. So to go from a bacterium to people is less of a step than to go from a mixture of amino acids to that bacterium."—Professor of Biology Lynn Margulis

## Classic but Questionable

Stanley Miller's experiment in 1953 is often cited as evidence that spontaneous generation could have happened in the past. The validity of his explanation, however, rests on the presumption that the earth's primordial atmosphere was "reducing." That means it contained only the smallest amount of free (chemically uncombined) oxygen. Why?

*The Mystery of Life's Origin: Reassessing Current Theories* points out that if much free oxygen was present, 'none of the amino acids could even be formed, and if by some chance they were, they would decompose quickly.'* How solid was Miller's presumption about the so-called primitive atmosphere?

In a classic paper published two years after his experiment, Miller wrote: "These ideas are of course speculation, for we do not know that the Earth had a reducing atmosphere when it was formed. . . . No direct evidence has yet been found."—*Journal of the American Chemical Society,* May 12, 1955.

Was evidence ever found? Some 25 years later, science writer Robert C. Cowen reported: "Scientists are having to rethink some of their assumptions. . . . Little evidence has emerged to support the notion of a hydrogen-rich, highly reducing atmosphere, but some evidence speaks against it."—*Technology Review,* April 1981.

And since then? In 1991, John Horgan wrote in *Scientific American:* "Over the past decade or so, doubts have grown about Urey and Miller's assumptions regarding the atmosphere. Laboratory experiments and computer-

---

* Oxygen is highly reactive. For example, it combines with iron and forms rust or with hydrogen and forms water. If there was much free oxygen in an atmosphere when amino acids were assembling, it would quickly combine with and dismantle the organic molecules as they formed.

ized reconstructions of the atmosphere . . . suggest that ultraviolet radiation from the sun, which today is blocked by atmospheric ozone, would have destroyed hydrogen-based molecules in the atmosphere. . . . Such an atmosphere [carbon dioxide and nitrogen] would not have been conducive to the synthesis of amino acids and other precursors of life."

Why, then, do many still hold that earth's early atmosphere was reducing, containing little oxygen? In *Molecular Evolution and the Origin of Life,* Sidney W. Fox and Klaus Dose answer: The atmosphere must have lacked oxygen because, for one thing, "laboratory experiments show that chemical evolution . . . would be largely inhibited by oxygen" and because compounds such as amino acids "are not stable over geological times in the presence of oxygen."

Is this not circular reasoning? The early atmosphere was a reducing one, it is said, because spontaneous generation of life could otherwise not have taken place. But there actually is no assurance that it was reducing.

There is another telling detail: If the gas mixture represents the atmosphere, the electric spark mimics lightning, and boiling water stands in for the sea, what or who does the scientist arranging and carrying out of the experiment represent?

## Right Hand, Left Hand

We know that there are right-handed and left-handed gloves. This is also true of amino acid molecules. Of some 100 known amino acids, only 20 are used in proteins, and all are left-handed ones. When scientists make amino acids in laboratories, in imitation of what they feel possibly occurred in a prebiotic soup, they find an equal number of right-handed and left-handed molecules. "This kind of 50-50 distribution," reports *The New York Times,* is "not characteristic of life, which depends on left-handed amino acids alone." Why living organisms are made up of only left-handed amino acids is "a great mystery." Even amino acids found in meteorites "showed excesses of left-handed forms." Dr. Jeffrey L. Bada, who studies problems involving the origin of life, said that "some influence outside the earth might have played some role in determining the handedness of biological amino acids."

be much more difficult than I, and most other people, envisioned." Other scientists share this change of mood. For example, back in 1969, Professor of Biology Dean H. Kenyon coauthored *Biochemical Predestination.* But more recently he concluded that it is "fundamentally implausible that unassisted matter and energy organized themselves into living systems."

Indeed, laboratory work bears out Kenyon's assessment that there is "a fundamental flaw in all current theories of the chemical origins of life." After Miller and others had synthesized amino acids, scientists set out to make proteins and DNA, both of which are necessary for life on earth. After thousands of experiments with so-called prebiotic conditions, what was the outcome? *The Mystery of Life's Origin: Reassessing Current Theories* notes: "There is an impressive contrast between the considerable success in synthesizing amino acids and the consistent failure to synthesize protein and DNA." The latter efforts are characterized by "uniform failure."

Realistically, the mystery encompasses more than how the first protein and nucleic acid (DNA or RNA) molecules came into existence. It includes how they work together. "It is only the partnership of the two molecules that makes contemporary life on Earth possible," says *The New Encyclopædia Britannica*. Yet the encyclopedia notes that how that partnership could come about remains "a critical and unsolved problem in the origin of life." True, indeed.

Appendix A, "Teamwork for Life" (pages 45-7), reviews some basic details of the intriguing teamwork between protein and nucleic acids in our cells. Even such a glimpse into the realm of our body cells elicits admiration for the work of scientists in this field. They have shed light on extraordinarily complex processes that few of us even think about but that operate every moment of our lives. From another standpoint, however, the staggering complexity and precision required returns us to the question, How did all of this come about?

You may know that origin-of-life scientists have not ceased trying to formulate a plausible scenario for the drama about the first appearance of life. Nevertheless, their new scripts are not proving to

> "These experiments . . . claim abiotic synthesis for what has in fact been produced and designed by highly intelligent and very much biotic man in an attempt to confirm ideas to which he was largely committed."
> —*Origin and Development of Living Systems.*

be convincing. (See Appendix B, "From 'the RNA World' or Another World?" page 48.) For example, Klaus Dose of the Institute for Biochemistry in Mainz, Germany, observed: "At present all discussions on principal theories and experiments in the field either end in stalemate or in a confession of ignorance."

Even at the 1996 International Conference on the Origin of Life, no solutions were forthcoming. Instead, the journal *Science* reported that the nearly 300 scientists who convened had "grappled with the riddle of how [DNA and RNA] molecules first appeared and how they evolved into self-reproducing cells."

Intelligence and advanced education were required to study and even begin to explain what occurs at the molecular level in our cells. Is it reasonable to believe that complicated steps occurred first in a "prebiotic soup," undirected, spontaneously, and by chance? Or was more involved?

### Why the Riddles?

A person today can look back over nearly half a century of speculation and thousands of attempts to prove that life originated on its own. If one does that, it would be hard to disagree with Nobel

## "A Deliberate Intellectual Act"

British astronomer Sir Fred Hoyle has spent decades studying the universe and life in it, even espousing that life on earth arrived from outer space. Lecturing at the California Institute of Technology, he discussed the order of amino acids in proteins.

"The big problem in biology," Hoyle said, "isn't so much the rather crude fact that a protein consists of a chain of amino acids linked together in a certain way, but that the explicit ordering of the amino acids endows the chain with remarkable properties . . . If amino acids were linked at random, there would be a vast number of arrangements that would be useless in serving the purposes of a living cell. When you consider that a  typical enzyme has a chain of perhaps 200 links and that there are 20 possibilities for each link, it's easy to see that the number of useless arrangements is enormous, more than the number of atoms in all the galaxies visible in the largest telescopes. This is for one enzyme, and there are upwards of 2000 of them, mainly serving very different purposes. So how did the situation get to where we find it to be?"

Hoyle added: "Rather than accept the fantastically small probability of life having arisen through the blind forces of nature, it seemed better to suppose that the origin of life was a deliberate intellectual act."

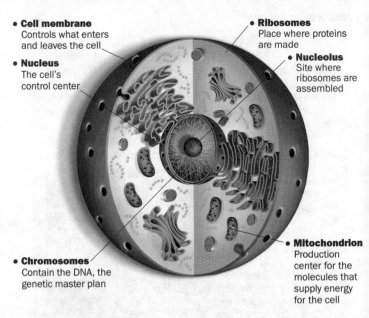

- **Cell membrane**
  Controls what enters and leaves the cell

- **Nucleus**
  The cell's control center

- **Chromosomes**
  Contain the DNA, the genetic master plan

- **Ribosomes**
  Place where proteins are made

- **Nucleolus**
  Site where ribosomes are assembled

- **Mitochondrion**
  Production center for the molecules that supply energy for the cell

*Even a glimpse into the complex world and intricate functions in each body cell leads to the question, How did all of this come about?*

laureate Francis Crick. Speaking about origin-of-life theories, Crick observed that there is "too much speculation running after too few facts." It is thus understandable that some scientists who examine the facts conclude that life is much too complex to pop up even in an organized laboratory, let alone in an uncontrolled environment.

If advanced science cannot prove that life could arise by itself, why do some scientists continue to hold to such theories? A few decades ago, Professor J. D. Bernal offered some insight in the book *The Origin of Life:* "By applying the strict canons of scientific method to this subject [the spontaneous generation of life], it is possible to demonstrate effectively at several places in the story, how life could not have arisen; the improbabilities are too great, the chances of the emergence of life too small." He added: "Regrettably from this point of view, life is here on Earth in all its multiplicity of forms and activities and the arguments have to be bent round to support its existence." And the picture has not improved.

Consider the underlying import of such reasoning. It is as much as saying: 'Scientifically it is correct to state that life cannot have begun by itself. But spontaneously arising life is the only possibility that we will consider. So it is necessary to bend the arguments to support the hypothesis that life arose spontaneously.' Are you comfortable with such logic? Does not such reasoning call for a lot of 'bending' of the facts?

There are, however, knowledgeable, respected scientists who do not see a need to bend facts to fit a prevailing philosophy on the origin of life. Rather, they permit the facts to point to a reasonable conclusion. What facts and what conclusion?

## Information and Intelligence

Interviewed in a documentary film, Professor Maciej Giertych, a noted geneticist from the Institute of Dendrology of the Polish Academy of Sciences, answered:

"We have become aware of the massive information contained in the genes. There is no known way to science how that information can arise spontaneously. It requires an intelligence; it cannot arise from chance events. Just mixing letters does not produce words." He added: "For example, the very complex DNA, RNA, protein replicating system in the cell must have been perfect from the very start. If not, life systems could not exist. The only logical explanation is that this vast quantity of information came from an intelligence."

The more you learn about the wonders of life, the more logical it is to agree with that conclusion: The origin of life requires an intelligent source. What source?

As noted earlier, millions of educated individuals conclude that life on earth must have been produced by a higher intelligence, a designer. Yes, after examining the matter fairly, they have accepted that even in our scientific age, it is reasonable to agree with the Biblical poet who long ago said about God: "For with you is the source of life." —Psalm 36:9.

Whether you have yet reached a firm conclusion about that or not, let us turn our attention to some wonders that involve you personally. Doing so is most satisfying and may shed considerable light on this matter that touches our lives.

---

Professor Michael J. Behe stated: "To a person who does not feel obliged to restrict his search to unintelligent causes, the straightforward conclusion is that many biochemical systems were designed. They were designed not by the laws of nature, not by chance and necessity; rather, they were *planned*. . . . Life on earth at its most fundamental level, in its most critical components, is the product of intelligent activity."

# APPENDIX A

## Teamwork for Life

Life could not exist on earth without the teamwork of protein and nucleic acid molecules (DNA or RNA) within a living cell. Let us briefly review some of the details of that intriguing molecular teamwork, for they are the reason why many find it hard to believe that living cells appeared by accident.

Peering into the human body, down to and even inside our microscopic cells, we find that we consist primarily of protein molecules. Most of these are made up of ribbonlike strips of amino acids that are bent and twisted into various shapes. Some fold into a ball, whereas others are shaped like accordion pleats.

Certain proteins work with fatlike molecules to form cell membranes. Others help carry oxygen from the lungs to the rest of our body. Some proteins act as enzymes (catalysts) to digest our food by splitting the proteins in the food into amino acids. Those are just a few of the thousands of tasks that proteins perform. You would be right in saying that proteins are the skilled workers of life; without them life would not exist. Proteins, in turn, would not exist were it not for their link with DNA. But what is DNA? What is it like? How is it linked with proteins? Brilliant scientists have won Nobel prizes for uncovering the answers. We, though, do not have to be advanced biologists to grasp the basics.

## The Master Molecule

Cells are largely made of proteins, so new proteins are constantly needed to maintain cells, to make new cells, and to facilitate chemical reactions within cells. The instructions needed for producing proteins are contained in the DNA (deoxyribonucleic acid) molecules. To understand better how protein is produced, take a closer look at DNA.

DNA molecules reside in the cell nucleus. In addition to carrying instructions necessary for the production of proteins, DNA stores and transmits genetic information from one generation of cells to the next. The shape of DNA molecules resembles a twisted rope ladder (termed a "double helix"). Each of the two strands in the DNA ladder consists of a vast number of smaller parts called nucleotides, which exist in one of four types: adenine (A), guanine (G), cytosine (C), and thymine (T). With this DNA "alphabet," a pair of letters—either A with

T or G with C—form one rung in the double-helix ladder. The ladder contains thousands of genes, the basic units of heredity.

A gene holds the information needed to build a protein. The sequence of letters in the gene forms a coded message, or blueprint, that tells what kind of protein should be built. Hence, the DNA, with all its subunits, is the master molecule of life. Without its coded instructions, diverse proteins could not exist—thus no life.

## The Go-Betweens

However, since the blueprint for building a protein is stored in the nucleus of the cell and the actual site for building proteins is outside the nucleus, help is needed to get the coded blueprint from the nucleus to the "building site." RNA (ribonucleic acid) molecules provide this help. RNA molecules are chemically similar to those of DNA, and several forms of RNA are needed to do the job. Take a closer look at these extremely complex processes for making our vital proteins with the help of RNA.

Work starts in the cell's nucleus, where a section of the DNA ladder unzips. This allows RNA letters to link to the exposed DNA letters of one of the DNA strands. An enzyme moves along the RNA letters to join them into a strand. Thus DNA letters are transcribed into RNA letters, forming what you might call a DNA dialect. The newly formed chain of RNA peels away, and the DNA ladder zips up again.

After further modification, this particular type of message-carrying RNA is ready. It moves out of the nucleus and heads for the protein-production site, where the RNA letters are decoded. Each set of three RNA letters forms a "word" that calls for one specific amino acid. Another form of RNA looks for that amino acid, grabs it with the help of an enzyme, and tows it to the "construction site." As the RNA sentence is being read and translated, a growing chain of amino acids is produced. This chain curls and folds into a unique shape, leading to one kind of protein. And there may well be over 50,000 kinds in our body.

Even this process of protein folding is significant. In 1996, scientists around the world, "armed with their best computer programs, competed to solve one of the most complex problems in biology: how a single protein, made from a long string of amino acids, folds itself into the intricate shape that determines the role it plays in life. . . . The result, succinctly put, was this: the computers lost and the proteins won. . . . Scientists have estimated that for an average-sized

protein, made from 100 amino acids, solving the folding problem by trying every possibility would take $10^{27}$ (a billion billion billion) years." —*The New York Times.*

We have considered only a summary of how a protein is formed, but you can see what an incredibly complex process it is. Have you an idea of how long it takes for a chain of 20 amino acids to form? About one second! And this process goes on constantly in our body cells, from our head to our foot and everywhere in between.

What is the point? While other factors too numerous to mention are involved, the teamwork needed to produce and maintain life is awe-inspiring. And the term "teamwork" hardly describes the precise interaction required to produce a protein molecule, since a protein needs information from DNA molecules, and DNA needs several forms of specialized RNA molecules. Nor can we ignore the various enzymes, each performing a distinct and vital role. As our body makes new cells, which happens billions of times a day and without our conscious guidance, it requires copies of all three components —DNA, RNA, and protein. You can see why the magazine *New Scientist* comments: "Take away any one of the three and life grinds to a halt." Or take this a step further. Without a complete and functioning team, life could not have come about.

Is it reasonable that each of those three molecular team players arose spontaneously at the same time, in the same place, and so precisely tuned that they could combine to work their wonders?

There is, though, an alternative explanation as to how life on earth came about. Many have come to believe that life was the careful product of a Designer with intelligence of the highest order.

# APPENDIX B

## From "the RNA World" or Another World?

In view of the DNA-RNA-protein team impasse, some researchers have offered "the RNA world" theory. What is that? Instead of asserting that DNA, RNA, and proteins originated simultaneously to produce life, they say that RNA by itself was the first spark of life. Is this theory sound?

In the 1980's, researchers discovered in their laboratory that RNA molecules could act as their own enzymes by snipping themselves in two and splicing themselves back together. So it was speculated that RNA might have been the first self-replicating molecule. It is theorized that in time, these RNA molecules learned to form cell membranes and that finally, the RNA organism gave rise to DNA. "The apostles of the RNA world," writes Phil Cohen in *New Scientist,* "believe that their theory should be taken, if not as gospel, then as the nearest thing to truth."

Not all scientists, though, accept this scenario. Skeptics, observes Cohen, "argued that it was too great a leap from showing that two RNA molecules partook in a bit of self mutilation in a test tube, to claiming that RNA was capable of running a cell single-handed and triggering the emergence of life on Earth."

There are other problems as well. Biologist Carl Woese holds that "the RNA world theory . . . is fatally flawed because it fails to explain where the energy came from to fuel the production of the first RNA molecules." And researchers have never located a piece of RNA that can replicate itself from scratch. There is also the issue of where RNA came from in the first place. Though "the RNA world" theory appears in many textbooks, most of it, says researcher Gary Olsen, "is speculative optimism."

Another theory that some scientists have espoused is that our planet was seeded with life that came from outer space. But this theory does not really address the question, What originated life? Saying that life comes from outer space, notes science writer Boyce Rensberger, "merely changes the location of the mystery." It does not explain the origin of life. It merely sidesteps the issue by relocating the origin to another solar system or galaxy. The real issue remains.

# CHAPTER FOUR

# How Unique You Are!

BEFORE starting your activities each morning, do you glance in a mirror to check your appearance? You may not have time to be contemplative then. But take a moment now to marvel at what is involved as you take such a simple glance.

Your eyes enable you to view yourself in full color, even though color vision is not vital to life. The position of your ears gives you stereophonic hearing; thus you can locate the source of sounds, such as the voice of a loved one. We may take that for granted, yet a book for sound engineers comments: "In considering the human hearing system in any depth, however, it is difficult to escape the conclusion that its intricate functions and structures indicate some beneficent hand in its design."

Your nose also manifests marvelous design. Through it you can breathe air, which keeps you alive. Also, it has millions of sense receptors, enabling you to discern some 10,000 nuances of smell. As you enjoy a meal, another sense comes into play. Thousands of taste buds convey flavors to you. Other receptors on your tongue help you to feel if your teeth are clean.

Yes, you have five senses—*sight, hearing, smell, taste,* and *touch.* Granted, some animals have keener night vision, more sensitive smell, or more acute hearing, but man's balance of these senses certainly allows him to excel in many ways.

Let us, though, consider *why* we can benefit from these abilities and capacities. All of them depend on the three-pound organ inside our head—our brain. Animals have functioning brains. Still, the human brain is in a class by itself, making us undeniably unique. How so? And how does this uniqueness relate to our interest in having a meaningful, lasting life?

### Your Marvelous Brain

For years man's brain has been likened to a computer, yet recent discoveries show that the comparison falls far short. "How does one begin to comprehend the functioning of an organ with somewhere in the neighborhood of 50 billion neurons with a million billion synapses (connections), and with an overall firing rate of perhaps 10 million billion times per second?" asked Dr. Richard M. Restak.

---

### Chess Champion Versus Computer

When the advanced computer Deep Blue vanquished the world champion chess player, the question arose, "Aren't we forced to conclude that Deep Blue must have a mind?"

Professor David Gelernter of Yale University replied: "No. Deep Blue is just a machine. It doesn't have a mind any more than a flowerpot has a mind. . . . Its chief meaning is this: that human beings are champion machine builders."

Professor Gelernter pointed to this major difference: "The brain is a machine that is capable of creating an 'I.' Brains can summon mental worlds into being, and computers can't."

He concluded: "The gap between human and [computer] is permanent and will never be closed. Machines will continue to make life easier, healthier, richer and more puzzling. And human beings will continue to care, ultimately, about the same things they always have: about themselves, about one another and, many of them, about God. On those terms, machines have never made a difference. And they never will."

---

His answer? "The performance of even the most advanced of the neural-network computers . . . has about one ten-thousandth the mental capacity of a housefly." Consider, then, how much a computer fails to measure up to a human brain, which is so remarkably superior.

What man-made computer can repair itself, rewrite its program, or improve over the years? When a computer system needs to be adjusted, a programmer must write and enter new coded instructions. Our brain does such work automatically, both in the

early years of life and in old age. You would not be
exaggerating to say that the most advanced computers are very primitive compared to the brain. Scientists have called it "the most complicated structure known" and "the most complex object in the
universe." Consider some discoveries that have led
many to conclude that the human brain is the product of a caring Creator.

## Use It or Lose It

Useful inventions such as cars and jet planes are
basically limited by the *fixed* mechanisms and elec-
trical systems that men design and install. By contrast, our brain is, at the very least, a highly *flexible*
biological mechanism or system. It can keep changing according to the way it is used—or abused. Two
main factors seem responsible for how our brain de-
velops throughout our lifetime—what we allow to
enter it through our senses and what we choose to
think about.

Although hereditary factors may have a role in
mental performance, modern research shows that
our brain is not fixed by our genes at the time of con-
ception. "No one suspected that the brain was as
changeable as science now knows it to be," writes
Pulitzer prize-winning author Ronald Kotulak. After interviewing more than 300 researchers, he concluded: "The brain is not a static organ; it is a constantly changing mass of cell connections that are
deeply affected by experience."—*Inside the Brain.*

Still, our experiences are not the only means of
shaping our brain. It is affected also by our thinking. Scientists find that the brains of people who re-

---

### Supercomputer Equals Snail

"Today's computers are not even close to a 4-year-old human in their ability to see, talk, move, or use common sense. One reason, of course, is sheer computing power. It has been estimated that the information processing capacity of even the most powerful supercomputer is equal to the nervous system of a snail—a tiny fraction of the power available to the supercomputer inside [our] skull."—Steven Pinker, director of the Center for Cognitive Neuroscience at the Massachusetts Institute of Technology.

---

main mentally active have up to 40 percent more connections (synapses) between nerve cells (neurons) than do the brains of the mentally lazy. Neuroscientists conclude: You have to use it or you lose it. What, though, of the elderly? There seems to be some loss of brain cells as a person ages, and advanced age can bring memory loss. Yet the difference is much less than was once believed. A *National Geographic* report on the human brain said: "Older people . . . retain capacity to generate new connections and to keep old ones via mental activity."

Recent findings about our brain's flexibility accord with advice found in the Bible. That book of wisdom urges readers to be 'transformed by making their mind over' or to be "made new" through "accurate knowledge" taken into the mind. (Romans 12:2; Colossians 3:10) Jehovah's Witnesses have seen this happen as people study the Bible and apply its counsel. Many thousands—from the whole spectrum of social and educational backgrounds—have done so. They remain distinct individuals, but they have become happier and more balanced, displaying what a first-century writer called "soundness of mind." (Acts 26:24, 25) Improvements like these result largely from one's making good use of a part of the cerebral cortex located in the front of the head.

## Your Frontal Lobe

Most neurons in the outer layer of the brain, the cerebral cortex, are not linked directly to muscles and sensory organs. For example, consider the billions of neurons that make up the frontal lobe. (See drawing, page 56.) Brain scans prove that the frontal lobe becomes active when you think of a word or call up memories. The front part of the brain plays a special role in your being you.

"The prefrontal cortex . . . is most involved with elaboration of thought, intelligence, motivation, and personality. It associates experiences necessary for the production of abstract ideas, judgment, persistence, planning, concern for others, and conscience. . . . It is the elaboration of this region that sets human beings apart from other animals." (Marieb's *Human Anatomy and Physiology*) We certainly see evidence of this distinction in what humans have accomplished in fields such as math-

---

"The human brain is composed almost exclusively of the [cerebral] cortex. The brain of a chimpanzee, for example, also has a cortex, but in far smaller proportions. The cortex allows us to think, to remember, to imagine. Essentially, we are human beings by virtue of our cortex."—Edoardo Boncinelli, director of research in molecular biology, Milan, Italy.

---

### From Particle Physics to Your Brain

Professor Paul Davies reflected on the ability of the brain to handle the abstract field of mathematics. "Mathematics is not something that you find lying around in your back yard. It's produced by the human mind. Yet if we ask where mathematics works best, it is in areas like particle physics and astrophysics, areas of fundamental science that are very, very far removed from everyday affairs." What does that imply? "It suggests to me that consciousness and our ability to do mathematics are no mere accident, no trivial detail, no insignificant by-product of evolution."—*Are We Alone?*

---

ematics, philosophy, and justice, which primarily involve the prefrontal cortex.

Why do humans have a large, flexible prefrontal cortex, which contributes to higher mental functions, whereas in animals this area is rudimentary or nonexistent? The contrast is so great that biologists who claim that we evolved speak of the "mysterious explosion in brain size." Professor of Biology Richard F. Thompson, noting the extraordinary expansion of our cerebral cortex, admits: "As yet we have no very clear understanding of why this happened." Could the reason lie in man's having been *created* with this peerless brain capacity?

### Unequaled Communication Skills

Other parts of the brain also contribute to our uniqueness. Behind our prefrontal cortex is a strip stretching across the head—the motor cortex. It contains billions of neurons that connect with our muscles. It too has features that contribute to our

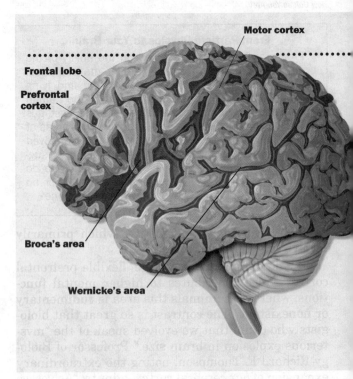

Motor cortex

Frontal lobe

Prefrontal cortex

Broca's area

Wernicke's area

being far different from apes or other animals. The primary motor cortex gives us "(1) an exceptional capability to use the hand, the fingers, and the thumb to perform highly dexterous manual tasks, and (2) use of the mouth, lips, tongue, and facial muscles to talk."—Guyton's *Textbook of Medical Physiology.*

Consider briefly how the motor cortex affects your ability to speak. Over half of it is devoted to the organs of communication. This helps to explain

the unparalleled communication skills of humans. Though our hands play a role in communication (in writing, normal gestures, or sign language), the mouth usually plays the major part. Human speech —from a baby's first word to the voice of an elderly person—is unquestionably a marvel. Some 100 muscles in the tongue, lips, jaw, throat, and chest cooperate to produce countless sounds. Note this contrast: One brain cell can direct 2,000 fibers of an athlete's calf muscle, but brain cells for the voice

---

**Every People Has One**

Throughout history, whenever one people encountered another, each found the other speaking a language. *The Language Instinct* comments: "No mute tribe has ever been discovered, and there is no record that a region has served as a 'cradle' of language from which it spread to previously languageless groups. . . . The universality of complex language is a discovery that fills linguists with awe, and is the first reason to suspect that language is . . . the product of a special human instinct."

---

box may concentrate on only 2 or 3 muscle fibers. Does that not suggest that our brain is specially equipped for communication?

Each short phrase that you utter requires a specific pattern of muscular movements. The meaning of a single expression can change depending upon the degree of movement and split-second timing of scores of different muscles. "At a comfortable rate," explains speech expert Dr. William H. Perkins, "we utter about 14 sounds per second. That's twice as fast as we can control our tongue, lips, jaw or any other parts of our speech mechanism when we move them separately. But put them all together for speech and they work the way fingers of expert typists and concert pianists do. Their movements overlap in a symphony of exquisite timing."

The actual information needed to ask the simple question, "How are you today?" is stored in a part of your brain's frontal lobe called Broca's area, which some consider to be your speech center. Nobel laureate neuroscientist Sir John Eccles wrote: "No area corresponding to the . . . speech area of Broca has been recognized in apes." Even if some similar areas are found in animals, the fact is that scientists cannot get apes to produce more than a few crude speech sounds. You, though, can produce complicated language. To do so, you put words together according to the grammar of your language. Broca's area helps you do that, both in speaking and in writing.

Of course, you cannot exercise the miracle of speech unless you know at least one language and understand what its words mean. This involves another special part of your brain, known as Wernicke's area. Here, billions of neurons discern the

---

### Language and Intelligence

Why does human intelligence far surpass that of animals, such as apes? A key is our use of syntax—putting sounds together to make words and using words to make sentences. Theoretical neurophysiologist Dr. William H. Calvin explains:

"Wild chimpanzees use about three dozen different vocalizations to convey about three dozen different meanings. They may repeat a sound to intensify its meaning, but they do not string together three sounds to add a new word to their vocabulary.

"We humans also use about three dozen vocalizations, called phonemes. Yet only their combinations have content: we string together meaningless sounds to make meaningful words." Dr. Calvin noted that "no one has yet explained" the leap from the animals' "one sound/one meaning" to our uniquely human capacity to use syntax.

## You Can Do More Than Doodle

"Is only man, *Homo sapiens,* capable of communicating by language? Clearly the answer must depend on what is meant by 'language'—for all the higher animals certainly communicate with a great variety of signs, such as gestures, odours, calls, cries and songs, and even the dance of the bees. Yet animals other than man do not appear to have structured grammatical language. And animals do not, which may be highly significant, draw representational pictures. At best they only doodle."—Professors R. S. and D. H. Fouts.

meaning of spoken or written words. Wernicke's area helps you to make sense of statements and to comprehend what you hear or read; thus you can learn information and can respond sensibly.

There is even more to your fluent speech. To illustrate: A verbal "Hello" can convey a host of meanings. Your tone of voice reflects whether you are happy, excited, bored, rushed, annoyed, sad, or frightened, and it may even reveal degrees of those emotional states. Another area of your brain supplies information for the emotional part of speech. So, various parts of your brain come into play when you communicate.

Chimpanzees have been taught some limited sign language, but their use of it is essentially limited to simple requests for food or other basics. Having worked to teach chimps simple nonverbal communication, Dr. David Premack concluded: "Human language is an embarrassment for evolutionary theory because it is vastly more powerful than one can account for."

We might ponder: 'Why do humans have this marvelous skill to communicate thoughts and feelings, to inquire and to respond?' *The Encyclopedia of Language and Linguistics* states that "[human] speech is special" and admits that "the search for precursors in animal communication does not help much in bridging the enormous gap that separates language and speech from nonhuman behaviors." Professor Ludwig Koehler summarized the difference: "Human speech is a secret; it is a divine gift, a miracle."

What a difference there is between an ape's use of signs and the complex language ability of children! Sir John Eccles referred to what most of us have also observed, an ability "exhibited even by 3-year-old children with their torrent of questions in their desire to understand their world." He added: "By contrast, apes do not ask questions." Yes, only humans form questions, including questions about the meaning of life.

### Memory and More!

When you glance in a mirror, you may think of how you looked when you were younger, even comparing that with what your appearance could be in the years to come or how you would look after applying cosmetics. These thoughts can arise almost

---

"Turning to the human mind, we also find structures of marvellous intricacy," notes Professor A. Noam Chomsky. "Language is a case in point, but not the only one. Think of the capacity to deal with abstract properties of the number system, [which seems] unique to humans."

---

### "Endowed" to Ask

Concerning the future of our universe, physicist Law-rence Krauss wrote: "We are emboldened to ask ques-tions about things we may never see directly because we *can* ask them. Our children, or their children, will one day answer them. We are endowed with imagination."

---

unconsciously, yet something very special is occur-ring, something that no animal can experience.

Unlike animals, who mainly live and act on pres-ent needs, humans can contemplate the past and plan for the future. A key to your doing that is the brain's almost limitless memory capacity. True, an-imals have a degree of memory, and thus they can find their way back home or recall where food may be. Human memory is far greater. One scientist es-timated that our brain can hold information that "would fill some twenty million volumes, as many as in the world's largest libraries." Some neuroscien-tists estimate that during an average life span, a person uses only 1/100 of 1 percent (.0001) of his po-tential brain capacity. You might well ask, 'Why do we have a brain with so much capacity that we hard-ly test a fraction of it in a normal lifetime?'

Nor is our brain just some vast storage place for information, like a supercomputer. Biology pro-fessors Robert Ornstein and Richard F. Thompson wrote: "The ability of the human mind to learn—to store and recall information—is the most remark-able phenomenon in the biological universe. Every-thing that makes us human—language, thought, knowledge, culture—is the result of this extraordi-nary capability."

*Only humans form questions.*
*Some are questions about the meaning of life*

Moreover, you have a *conscious* mind. That statement may seem basic, but it sums up something that unquestionably makes you exceptional. The mind has been described as "the elusive entity where intelligence, decision making, perception, awareness and sense of self reside." As creeks, streams, and rivers feed into a sea, so memories, thoughts, images, sounds, and feelings flow constantly into or through our mind. Consciousness, says one definition, is "the perception of what passes in a man's own mind."

Modern researchers have made great strides in understanding the physical makeup of the brain and some of the electrochemical processes that occur in it. They can also explain the circuitry and

*Unlike the animals, humans have an
awareness about themselves and about the future*

functioning of an advanced computer. However, there is a vast difference between brain and computer. With your brain you are conscious and are aware of your being, but a computer certainly is not. Why the difference?

Frankly, how and why consciousness arises from physical processes in our brain is a mystery. "I don't see how any science can explain that," one neurobiologist commented. Also, Professor James Trefil observed: "What, exactly, it means for a human being to be conscious . . . is the only major question in the sciences that we don't even know how to ask." One reason why is that scientists are using the brain to try to understand the brain. And just studying the physiology of the brain may not be enough. Consciousness is "one of the most profound mysteries of existence," observed Dr. David Chalmers, "but knowledge of the brain alone may not get [scientists] to the bottom of it."

Nonetheless, each of us experiences consciousness. For example, our vivid memories of past events are not mere stored facts, like computer bits of information. We can reflect on our experiences, draw lessons from them, and use them to shape our future. We are able to consider several future scenarios and evaluate the possible effects of each. We have the capacity to analyze, create, appreciate, and love. We can enjoy pleasant conversations about the past, present, and future. We have ethical values about behavior and can use them in making decisions that may or may not be of immediate benefit. We are attracted to beauty in art and morals. In our mind we can mold and refine our ideas and guess how other people will react if we carry these out.

Such factors produce an awareness that sets humans apart from other life-forms on earth. A dog, a cat, or a bird looks in a mirror and responds as if seeing another of its kind. But when you look in a mirror, you are conscious of yourself as a being with the capacities just mentioned. You can reflect on dilemmas, such as: 'Why do some turtles live 150 years and some trees live over 1,000 years, but an intelligent human makes the news if he reaches 100?' Dr. Richard Restak states: "The human brain, and the human brain alone, has the capacity to step back, survey its own operation, and thus achieve some degree of transcendence. Indeed, our capacity for rewriting our own script and redefining ourselves in the world is what distinguishes us from all other creatures in the world."

Man's consciousness baffles some. The book *Life Ascending,* while favoring a mere biological explanation, admits: "When we ask how a process [evolution] that resembles a game of chance, with dreadful penalties for the losers, could have generated such qualities as love of beauty and truth, compassion, freedom, and, above all, the expansiveness of the human spirit, we are perplexed. The more we ponder our spiritual resources, the more our wonder deepens." Very true. Thus, we might round out our view of human uniqueness by a few evidences of our consciousness that illustrate why many are convinced that there must be an intelligent Designer, a Creator, who cares for us.

### Art and Beauty

"Why do people pursue art so passionately?" asked Professor Michael Leyton in *Symmetry, Causality, Mind.* As he pointed out, some might say that mental activity such as mathematics confers clear benefits to humans, but why art? Leyton illustrated his point by saying that people travel great distances to art exhibits and concerts. What inner sense is involved? Similarly, people around the globe put attractive pictures or paintings on the walls of their home or office. Or consider music. Most people like to listen to some style of music at

home and in their cars. Why? It certainly is not because music once contributed to the survival of the fittest. Says Leyton: "Art is perhaps the most inexplicable phenomenon of the human species."

Still, we all know that enjoying art and beauty is part of what makes us feel "human." An animal might sit on a hill and look at a colorful sky, but is it drawn to beauty as such? We look at a mountain torrent shimmering in the sunshine, stare at the dazzling diversity in a tropical rain forest, gaze at a palm-lined beach, or admire the stars sprinkled across the black velvety sky. Often we feel awed, do we not? Beauty of that sort makes our hearts glow, our spirits soar. Why?

Why do we have an innate craving for things that, in reality, contribute little materially to our survival? From where do our aesthetic values come? If we do not take into account a Maker who shaped these values at man's creation, these questions lack satisfying answers. This is also true regarding beauty in morals.

## Moral Values

Many recognize the highest form of beauty to be fine deeds. For instance, being loyal to principles in the face of persecution, acting unselfishly to relieve others' suffering, and forgiving someone who hurt us are actions that appeal to the moral sense of thinking people everywhere. This is the kind of beauty mentioned in the ancient Biblical proverb: "The insight of a man certainly slows down his anger, and it is beauty on his part to pass over transgression." Or as another proverb observes: "The desirable thing in earthling man is his loving-kindness."—Proverbs 19:11, 22.

We all know that some people, and even groups, ignore or trample on elevated morals, but the majority do not. From what source do the moral values found in virtually all areas and in all periods come? If there is no Source of morality, no Creator, did right and wrong simply originate with people, human society? Consider an example: Most individuals and groups hold murder to be wrong. But one could ask, 'Wrong in comparison to what?' Obviously there is some sense of morality that underlies human society in general and that has been incorporated into the laws of many lands. What is the source of this standard of morality? Could it

If the universe and our being alive in it are accidental, our lives can have no *lasting* meaning. But if our life in the universe results from design, there must be a satisfying meaning to it.

not be an intelligent Creator who has moral values and who placed the faculty of conscience, or ethical sense, in humans?—Compare Romans 2:14, 15.

### You Can Contemplate the Future and Plan for It

Another facet of human consciousness is our ability to consider the future. When asked whether humans have traits that distinguish them from animals, Professor Richard Dawkins acknowledged that man has, indeed, unique qualities. After mentioning "the ability to plan ahead using conscious, imagined foresight," Dawkins added: "Short-term benefit has always been the only thing that counts in evolution; long-term benefit has never counted. It has never been possible for something to evolve in spite of being bad for the immediate short-term good of the individual. For the first time ever, it's possible for at least some people to say, 'Forget about the fact that you can make a short-term profit by chopping down this forest; what about the long-term benefit?' Now I think that's genuinely new and unique."

Other researchers confirm that humans' ability for conscious, long-term planning is without parallel. Neurophysiologist William H. Calvin notes: "Aside from hormonally triggered preparations for winter and mating, animals exhibit surprisingly little evidence of planning more than a few minutes

*Humans uniquely appreciate beauty,
think about the future, and are drawn to a Creator*

ahead." Animals may store food before a cold sea-
son, but they do not think things through and plan.
By contrast, humans consider the future, even the
distant future. Some scientists contemplate what
may happen to the universe billions of years hence.
Did you ever wonder why man—so different from
animals—is able to think about the future and lay
out plans?

The Bible says of humans: "Even time indefinite
[the Creator] has put in their heart." The *Revised
Standard Version* renders it: "He has put eternity
into man's mind." (Ecclesiastes 3:11) We use this
distinctive ability daily, even in as common an act

as glancing in a mirror and thinking what our appearance will be in 10 or 20 years. And we are confirming what Ecclesiastes 3:11 says when we give even passing thought to such concepts as the infinity of time and space. The mere fact that we have this ability harmonizes with the comment that a Creator has put "eternity into man's mind."

### Drawn to a Creator

Many people, however, are not satisfied fully by enjoying beauty, doing good to fellowmen, and thinking about the future. "Strangely enough," notes Professor C. Stephen Evans, "even in our most happy and treasured moments of love, we often feel something is missing. We find ourselves wanting more but not knowing what is the more we want." Indeed, conscious humans—unlike the animals with which we share this planet—feel another need.

"Religion is deeply rooted in human nature and experienced at every level of economic status and educational background." This summed up the research that Professor Alister Hardy presented in *The Spiritual Nature of Man*. It confirms what numerous other studies have established—man is God-conscious. While individuals may be atheists, whole nations are not. The book *Is God the Only Reality?* observes: "The religious quest for meaning . . . is the common experience in every culture and every age since the emergence of humankind."

From where does this seemingly inborn awareness of God come? If man were merely an accidental

---

### From Dodging Saber-Toothed Tigers?

John Polkinghorne, of the University of Cambridge, England, observed:

"Theoretical physicist Paul Dirac discovered something called quantum field theory which is fundamental to our understanding of the physical world. I can't believe Dirac's ability to discover that theory, or Einstein's ability to discover the general theory of relativity, is a sort of spin-off from our ancestors having to dodge saber-toothed tigers. Something much more profound, much more mysterious, is going on. . . .

"When we look at the rational order and transparent beauty of the physical world, revealed through physical science, we see a world shot through with signs of mind. To a religious believer, it is the mind of the Creator that is being discerned in that way."—*Commonweal.*

---

grouping of nucleic acid and protein molecules, why would these molecules develop a love of art and beauty, turn religious, and contemplate eternity?

Sir John Eccles concluded that an evolutionary explanation of man's existence "fails in a most important respect. It cannot account for the existence of each one of us as unique self-conscious beings." The more we learn about the workings of our brain and mind, the easier it is to see why millions of people have concluded that man's conscious existence is evidence of a Creator who cares about us.

In the next chapter, we will see why people of all walks of life have found that this rational conclusion lays the basis for finding satisfying answers to the vital questions, Why are we here, and where are we going?

# CHAPTER FIVE

# The Handiwork—What Is Behind It?

AS NOTED in earlier chapters, modern scientific discoveries offer an abundance of convincing evidence that the universe and life on earth both had a beginning. What caused their beginning?

After studying the available evidence, many have concluded that there must be a First Cause. Nonetheless, they may shy away from attaching personality to this Cause. Such reluctance to speak of a Creator mirrors the attitude of some scientists.

For instance, Albert Einstein was convinced that the universe had a beginning, and he expressed his desire "to know how God created the world." Yet Einstein did not admit to belief in a personal God; he spoke of a cosmic "religious feeling, which knows no dogma and no God conceived in man's image." Similarly, Nobel laureate chemist Kenichi Fukui expressed belief in a great framework in the universe. He said that "this great link and framework may be expressed in words such as 'Absolute' or 'God.'" But he called it an "idiosyncrasy of nature."

Are you aware that such belief in an impersonal cause parallels much of the Eastern religious thinking? Many Orientals believe that nature came into existence on its own. This idea is even expressed in the Chinese characters for nature, which literally mean "becomes by itself" or "self-existing." Einstein believed that his cosmic religious feeling was well expressed in Buddhism. Buddha held that it was not important whether a Creator had a hand in bringing forth the universe and humans. Similarly, Shinto provides no explanation of how nature came to be, and Shintoists believe that the gods are spirits of the dead that may assimilate with nature.

Interestingly, such thinking is not far removed from views that were popular in ancient Greece. The philosopher Epicurus (341-270 B.C.E.) is said to have believed that 'gods are too remote to do you any more harm than good.' He held that man is a product of nature, probably through spontaneous generation and the natural selection of the fittest. You may sense from this that similar ideas today are by no means modern.

Alongside the Epicureans were the Greek Stoics, who gave nature the position of God. They supposed that when humans die, impersonal energy from them is reabsorbed into the ocean of energy making up God. They felt that cooperating with natural laws was the supreme good. Have you heard similar views in our day?

### Contest Over a Personal God

Nevertheless, we should not dismiss all information from ancient Greece as quaint history. In the context of such beliefs, a noted teacher in the first century presented one of history's most significant speeches. The physician and historian Luke recorded this speech, and we find it in chapter 17 of the book Acts of Apostles. It can help us to settle our view of the First Cause and to see where we fit

*Many Orientals believe that nature came into existence by itself*

into the picture. How, though, can a speech given 1,900 years ago affect lives today as sincere individuals search for meaning in life?

That famous teacher, Paul, was invited to a high court in Athens. He there faced Epicureans and Stoics, who did not believe in a personal God. In his opening remarks, Paul mentioned seeing in their city an altar inscribed "To an Unknown God" (Greek, *A·gno'stoi The·oi'*). Interestingly, some think that biologist Thomas H. Huxley (1825-95) alluded to this when he coined the term "agnostic." Huxley applied the word to those who hold that "the ultimate cause (God) and the essential nature of things are unknown or unknowable." But is the Creator really "unknowable" as many have held?

That, frankly, is a misapplication of Paul's phrase; it misses Paul's point. Rather than saying that the Creator was unknowable, Paul was simply saying that He was unknown to those Athenians. Paul did not have at hand as much scientific evidence for the existence of a Creator as we do today.

*Paul made a thought-provoking speech about God while
standing on this hill, with the Acropolis in the background*

Still, Paul had no doubt that there is a personal, intelligent Designer whose qualities should draw us
to him. Note what Paul went on to say:

"What you are unknowingly giving godly devotion
to, this I am publishing to you. The God that made
the world and all the things in it, being, as this One
is, Lord of heaven and earth, does not dwell in hand-
made temples, neither is he attended to by human
hands as if he needed anything, because he himself
gives to all persons life and breath and all things.
And he made out of one man every nation of men,
to dwell upon the entire surface of the earth." (Acts

17:23-26) An interesting line of reasoning, do you not agree?

Yes, rather than suggesting that God was unknowable, Paul was emphasizing that those who made the Athenian altar, as well as many in his audience, did not yet know Him. Paul then urged them —and all who have since read his speech—to seek to know the Creator, for "he is not far off from each one of us." (Acts 17:27) You can see that Paul tactfully introduced the fact that we can see evidence of a Creator of all things by observing his creation. By doing this, we can also discern some of his qualities.

We have examined various lines of evidence that point to a Creator. One is the vast, intelligently organized universe, which clearly had a beginning. Another is life on earth, including the design manifest in our body cells. And a third is our brain, with our associated awareness of self and our interest in the future. But let us look first at two other examples of the Creator's handiwork that touch us daily. In doing so, ask yourself, 'What does this show me about the personality of the One who designed and provided it?'

## Learning From His Handiwork

Sheer observation of his creation tells much about the Creator. Paul, on another occasion, mentioned an example of this when he told a crowd in Asia Minor: "In the past generations [the Creator] permitted all the nations to go on in their ways, although, indeed, *he did not leave himself without witness* in that he did good, giving you rains from heaven and fruitful seasons, filling your hearts to the full with food and good cheer." (Acts 14:16, 17) Note the example Paul gave of how the Creator, in providing food for mankind, has borne witness to His personality.

In some lands today, people may take for granted the availability of food. Elsewhere, many struggle to get enough to eat. In either case, even the possibility of having any sustaining food depends on the wisdom and goodness of our Creator.

Food for both man and animals results from intricate cycles—including the water cycle, the carbon cycle, the phosphorus cycle, and the nitrogen cycle. It is general knowledge that in the vital process of photosynthesis, plants use carbon dioxide and water as raw materials to produce sugars, using sunlight as the energy source. Incidentally, during photosynthesis plants release oxygen. Could this be

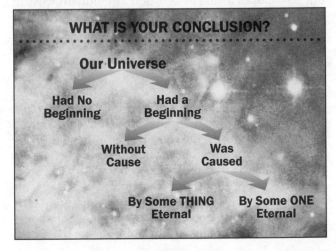

**WHAT IS YOUR CONCLUSION?**

Our Universe

Had No Beginning    Had a Beginning

Without Cause    Was Caused

By Some THING Eternal    By Some ONE Eternal

termed a "waste product"? To us this by-product is hardly waste. It is absolutely essential that we breathe in oxygen and use it to metabolize, or burn, food in our body. We exhale the resulting carbon dioxide, which plants recycle as a raw material for photosynthesis. We may have studied this process in a basic science class, but it is no less vital and marvelous. And this is just the start.

In our body cells and in those of animals, phosphorus is vital for transferring energy. From where do we get our phosphorus? Again, from plants. They absorb inorganic phosphates from the soil and convert them into organic phosphates. We consume plants containing phosphorus in these forms and use it for vital activities. Thereafter, the phosphorus returns to the soil in the form of body "wastes" that can again be absorbed by plants.

We also need nitrogen, which is part of every

---

### A Reasonable Conclusion

There is wide agreement among scientists that the universe had a beginning. Most also agree that before that beginning, something real must have existed. Some scientists talk about ever-existing energy. Others postulate a primordial chaos as the preexisting condition. Whatever terms are used, most presuppose the existence of something—something without a beginning—that extended back infinitely.

So the issue comes down to whether we presuppose some *thing* eternal or some *one* eternal. After considering what science has learned about the origin and nature of the universe and life on it, which of these alternatives seems more reasonable to you?

> "Each of the elements central to life—carbon, nitrogen, sulfur—is converted by bacteria from an inorganic, gaseous compound into a form that can be used by plants and animals."—*The New Encyclopædia Britannica.*

protein and DNA molecule in our body. How do we obtain this element that is so essential for life? Although about 78 percent of the air around us is nitrogen, neither plants nor animals can absorb it directly. So nitrogen in the air must be converted into other forms before it can be taken in by plants and later utilized by humans and animals. How does that conversion, or fixation, occur? In various ways. One way is by the action of lightning.* Nitrogen fixation is also accomplished by bacteria that live in nodules on the roots of legumes, such as peas, soybeans, and alfalfa. These bacteria convert atmospheric nitrogen into substances that plants can use. In this way, when you eat green vegetables, you take in nitrogen, which your body needs in order to produce proteins. Amazingly, we find species of legumes in tropical rain forests, deserts, and even tundras. And if an area is burned over, legumes usually are the first plants to recolonize.

What marvelous recycling systems these are! Each of them puts to good use wastes from the other cycles. The energy needed comes principally from our sun—a clean, endless, and steady source.

---

* Lightning transforms some nitrogen into an absorbable form, which falls to earth with the rain. Plants use this as a naturally provided fertilizer. After humans and animals consume plants and use this nitrogen, it returns to the soil as ammonium compounds and some eventually converts back into nitrogen gas.

How that contrasts with human efforts to recycle resources! Even man-made products that are called environmentally friendly may not contribute to a cleaner planet because of the complexity of human recycling systems. In this regard, *U.S. News & World Report* pointed out that products should be designed so that their high-value components can easily be recovered by recycling. Is that not what we observe in these natural cycles? So, what does this reveal about the Creator's forethought and wisdom?

## Impartial and Just

To help us see further some of the Creator's qualities, let us consider one more system—the immune system in our body. It also involves bacteria.

"Although human interest in bacteria frequently focuses on their harmful effects," observes *The New Encyclopædia Britannica,* "most bacteria are harmless to human beings, and many of them are actually beneficial." Indeed, they are of life-and-death importance. Bacteria play a crucial role in the nitrogen cycle just mentioned, as well as in cycles involving carbon dioxide and some elements. And we also need bacteria in our digestive tract. We have some 400 species in our lower intestinal tract alone, and they help to synthesize vitamin K and process wastes. Of further benefit to us, bacteria help cows turn grasses into milk. Other bacteria are vital in fermentation—in our making cheese, yogurt, pickles, sauerkraut, and kimchi. What, though, if bacteria get where they do not belong in our body?

Then up to two trillion white blood cells in our body fight the bacteria that might harm us. Daniel

E. Koshland, Jr., editor of *Science* magazine, explains: "The immune system is designed to recognize foreign invaders. To do so it generates on the order of $10^{11}$ [100,000,000,000] different kinds of immunological receptors so that no matter what the shape or form of the foreign invader there will be some complementary receptor to recognize it and effect its elimination."

One type of cell that our body uses to fight invaders is the macrophage; its name means "big eater," which is fitting because it devours foreign substances in our blood. For example, after eating an invading virus, the macrophage breaks it into small fragments. It then displays some protein from the virus. This bit of marker protein serves as a red flag to our immune system, sounding the alarm that foreign organisms are on the loose inside us. If another cell in the immune system, the helper T cell, recognizes the virus protein, it exchanges chemical signals with the macrophage. These chemicals are themselves extraordinary proteins that have a bewildering array of functions, regulating and boosting our immune system's response to invasion. This process results in a vigorous fight against the specific type of virus. Thus, we usually manage to overcome infections.

Actually, much more is involved, but even this brief description reveals the complexity of our immune system. How did we get this intricate mechanism? It came free of charge, regardless of our family's financial or social standing. Compare that with the inequity in health care available to most people. "For WHO [World Health Organization], growing inequity is literally a matter of life and death, since the poor pay the price of social inequality with their health," wrote the director general of WHO, Dr. Hiroshi Nakajima. You can understand this lament made by one of São Paulo's slum dwellers: "For us, good health care is like an item in a window display in a luxurious shopping mall. We can look at

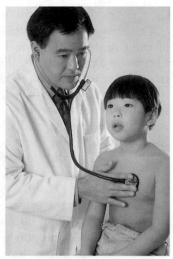

*God gave to each of us an immune system that surpasses anything modern medicine can provide*

it, but it is beyond our reach." Millions of people around the globe feel the same way.

Such inequities moved Albert Schweitzer to go to Africa to provide medical care for the less privileged, and his efforts earned him a Nobel prize. What qualities do you associate with men and women who have done similar good deeds? You probably realize that they have love for humanity and a sense of justice, believing that people in developing lands too are entitled to medical care. What, then, about the Provider of the wonderful immune system built into us regardless of financial and social standing? Does it not more significantly bespeak the Creator's sense of love, impartiality, and justice?

## Getting to Know the Creator

The above-noted systems are just basic examples of the Creator's handiwork, but do they not reveal him to be a real and intelligent person whose qualities and ways draw us to him? Numerous other examples could be considered. We have probably found in daily life, however, that merely observing a person's works may not really be enough for us to know him well. It would even be possible to misunderstand him if we did not gain a complete picture of him! And if that person has been misrepresented or maligned, would it not be good to meet him and hear his side? We might converse with him to find out how he reacts under different circumstances and what qualities he displays.

Of course, we cannot have a face-to-face conversation with the powerful Creator of the universe. Yet, he has revealed much about himself as a real person in a book that is available, in whole or in part, in more than 2,000 languages, including yours. That book—the Bible—invites you to get to know and cultivate a relationship with the Creator: "Draw close to God," it says, "and he will draw close to you." It also shows how it is possible to become his friend. (James 2:23; 4:8) Would you be interested in that?

To this end, we invite you to consider the Creator's factual and fascinating account of his creative activities.

# CHAPTER SIX

# An Ancient Creation Record —Can You Trust It?

"WHO can say whence it all came, and how creation happened?" You find that question in the poem "The Song of Creation." Composed in Sanskrit over 3,000 years ago, it is part of the *Rig-Veda,* a Hindu holy book. The poet doubted that even the many Hindu gods could know "how creation happened" because "the gods themselves are *later* than creation."—Italics ours.

Writings from Babylon and Egypt offer similar myths about the birth of their gods in a universe that already existed. A key point, however, is that those myths could not say where the original universe came from. You will find, though, that one creation record is different. This particular record, the Bible, opens with the words: "In the beginning God created the heavens and the earth."—Genesis 1:1.

Moses wrote that simple, dramatic statement some 3,500 years ago. It focuses on a Creator, God, who transcends the material universe because he made it and hence existed before it was. The same book teaches that "God is a Spirit," which means he exists in a form that our eyes cannot see. (John 4: 24) Such an existence is perhaps more conceivable today, since scientists have described powerful neutron stars and black holes in space—invisible objects that are detectable by the effects they produce.

Significantly, the Bible reports: "There are heavenly bodies, and earthly bodies; but the glory of the heavenly bodies is one sort, and that of the earthly

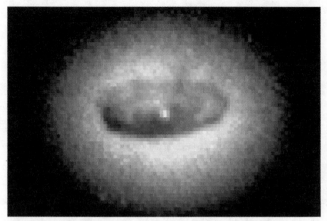

*Dust disks, such as this one in galaxy NGC 4261, are evidence of powerful black holes, which cannot be seen. The Bible reports the existence, in another realm, of creatures that are powerful but cannot be seen*

bodies is a different sort." (1 Corinthians 15:40, 44) That does not refer to the invisible cosmic matter that astronomers study. The "heavenly bodies" mentioned are intelligent spirit bodies. 'Who, besides the Creator,' you may wonder, 'has a spirit body?'

### Invisible Heavenly Creatures

According to the Biblical record, the visible realm was not the first thing created. This ancient creation account reports that the first step of creation was the bringing into existence of another spirit person, the firstborn Son. He was "the firstborn of all creation," or "the beginning of the creation by God." (Colossians 1:15; Revelation 3:14) This first created individual was unique.

He was the only creation that God produced directly, and he was endowed with great wisdom. In fact, a later writer, a king renowned for his own wisdom, described this Son as "a master worker," who was employed in all subsequent creative works. (Proverbs 8:22, 30; see also Hebrews 1:1, 2.) Of him the first-century teacher named Paul wrote: "By means of him all other things were created in the heavens and upon the earth, the things visible and the things invisible."—Colossians 1:16; compare John 1:1-3.

What are the invisible things in the heavens that the Creator brought into existence by means of this Son? While astronomers report billions of stars and invisible black holes, here the Bible is referring to hundreds of millions of spirit creatures—with spirit bodies. 'Why,' some may ask, 'create such invisible, intelligent beings?'

Just as a study of the universe can answer some questions about its Cause, a study of the Bible can provide us with important information about its Author. For instance, the Bible tells us that he is "the happy God," whose intentions and actions reflect love. (1 Timothy 1:11; 1 John 4:8) We can logically conclude, then, that God chose to have the association of other intelligent spirit persons who could also enjoy life. Each would have satisfying work that was mutually beneficial and would contribute to the Creator's purpose.

Nothing suggests that these spirit creatures were to be like robots in obeying God. Rather, he endowed them with intelligence and free will. Biblical accounts indicate that God encourages freedom of thought and freedom of action—confident that these pose no permanent threat to peace and harmony in the universe. Paul, using the personal name for the Creator, as found in the Hebrew Bible, wrote: "Now Jehovah is the Spirit; and where the spirit of Jehovah is, there is freedom."—2 Corinthians 3:17.

## Visible Things in the Heavens

What are the visible things that God created through his firstborn Son? They include our sun and all the other billions of stars and materials that make up the universe. Does the Bible give us any idea as to how God produced all of these out of nothing? Let us see by looking at the Bible in the light of modern science.

In the 18th century, the scientist Antoine-Laurent Lavoisier studied the weight of matter. He noticed that after a chemical reaction, the weight of the product equaled the combined weight of the original ingredients. For example, if paper is burned in oxygen, the resulting ash and gases weigh the same as the original paper and oxygen. Lavoisier proposed a law—'conservation of mass, or matter.' In 1910, *The Encyclopædia Britannica* explained: "Matter can neither be created nor destroyed." That seemed reasonable, at least back then.

However, the explosion of an atom bomb over the Japanese city of Hiroshima in 1945 publicly exposed a flaw in Lavoisier's law. During such an explosion of a supercritical mass of uranium, different types of matter form, but their combined mass is less than that of the original uranium. Why the loss? It is because some of the mass of the uranium is converted into an awesome flash of energy.

*Experiments supported the scientific theory that mass can be converted into energy and energy into mass*

Another problem with Lavoisier's law on the conservation of matter arose in 1952 with the detonation of a thermonuclear device (hydrogen bomb). In that explosion, hydrogen atoms combined to form helium. The mass of the resulting helium, though, was less than that of the original hydrogen. A portion of the mass of the hydrogen was converted into explosive energy, an explosion far more devastating than the bomb released over Hiroshima.

As these explosions proved, a small amount of matter represents an enormous quantity of energy. This link between matter and energy explains the power of the sun, which keeps us alive and well. What is the link? Well, some 40 years earlier, in 1905, Einstein had predicted a relationship between matter and energy. Many know of his equation $E=mc^2$.* Once Einstein formulated that relationship, other scientists could explain how the sun has kept shining for billions of years. Within the sun, there are continuous thermonuclear reactions. In this way, every second, the sun converts about 564 million tons of hydrogen into 560 million tons of helium. This means that some 4 million tons of matter are transformed into solar energy, a fraction of which reaches earth and sustains life.

Significantly, the reverse process is also possible. "Energy changes into matter when subatomic particles collide at high speeds and create new, heavier particles," explains *The World Book Encyclopedia*. Scientists accomplish this on a limited scale using huge machines called particle accelerators, in which subatomic particles collide at fantastic speeds, creating matter. "We're repeating one of the miracles of the universe—transforming energy into matter," explains Nobel laureate physicist Dr. Carlo Rubbia.

'True,' one may say, 'but what does this have to do with the record of creation that I can read in the Bible?' Well, the Bible is not a scientific textbook as such, yet it has proved to be up-to-date and in harmony with scientific facts. From beginning to end, the Bible points to the One who created all the matter in the universe, *the* Scientist. (Nehemiah 9:6; Acts 4:24; Revelation 4:11) And it clearly shows the relationship between energy and matter.

For example, the Bible invites readers to do this: "Raise your eyes high up and see. Who has creat-

---

* Energy equals mass multiplied by the speed of light squared.

ed these things? It is the One who is bringing forth the army of them even by number, all of whom he calls even by name. Due to the abundance of dynamic energy, he also being vigorous in power, not one of them is missing." (Isaiah 40:26) Yes, the Bible is saying that a source of tremendous dynamic energy—the Creator—caused the material universe to come into existence. This is completely in harmony with modern technology. For this reason alone, the Biblical record of creation merits our deep respect.

After creating in the heavens things both invisible and visible, the Creator and his firstborn Son focused on the earth. Where did it come from? The variety of chemical elements making up our planet could have been produced directly by God's transforming unlimited dynamic energy into matter, which physicists today say is feasible. Or, as many scientists believe, the earth could have been formed out of matter ejected from the explosion of a supernova. Then again, who is to say whether there might have been a combination of methods, those just mentioned and others that scientists have not yet unraveled? Whatever the mechanism, the Creator is the dynamic Source of the elements that make up our earth, including all the minerals that are essential for keeping us alive.

You can appreciate that founding the earth would have involved much more than supplying all the materials in the correct proportions. Earth's size, its rotation, and its distance from the sun, as well as the inclination of its axis and the nearly circular shape of its orbit around the sun, also had to be just right—exactly as they are. Clearly, the Creator set in operation natural cycles that make our planet fit to support an abundance of life. We have every right to be amazed at it all. But imagine the reaction of heavenly spirit sons as they watched the producing of the earth and life upon it! One Bible book says that they "joyfully cried out together" and "began shouting in applause."—Job 38:4, 7.

## Understanding Genesis Chapter 1

The first chapter of the Bible gives partial details of some vital steps that God took to prepare the earth for human enjoyment. The chapter does not give every detail; as we read it, we should not be put off if it omits particulars that ancient readers could not have comprehended anyway. For example, in writing that chapter, Moses did not report the function of microscopic algae or bacteria. Such forms of life first came into human view after the invention of the microscope, in the 16th century. Nor did Moses specifically report on dinosaurs, whose existence was deduced from fossils in the 19th century. Instead, Moses was inspired to use words that could be understood by people of his day—but words that were accurate in all they said about earth's creation.

As you read Genesis chapter 1, from verse 3 onward, you will see that it is divided into six creative "days." Some claim that these were literal 24-hour days, meaning that the entire universe and life on earth were created in less than a week! However, you can easily discover that the Bible does not teach that. The book of Genesis was written in Hebrew. In that language, "day" refers to a period of time. It can be either a lengthy one or a literal day of 24 hours. Even in Genesis all six "days" are spoken of collectively as one lengthy period—'the day in which Jehovah made earth and heaven.' (Genesis 2:4; compare 2 Peter 3:8.) The fact is, the Bible reveals that the creative "days," or ages, encompass thousands of years.

A person can see this from what the Bible says about the seventh "day." The record of each of the first six "days" ends saying, 'and there came to be evening and morning, a first day,' and so on. Yet, you will not find that comment after the record of the seventh "day." And in the first century C.E., some 4,000 years downstream in history, the Bible referred to the seventh rest "day" as still continuing. (Hebrews 4:4-6) So the seventh "day" was a period spanning thousands of years, and we can logically conclude the same about the first six "days."

### The First and Fourth "Days"

It seems that the earth had been established in orbit around the sun and was a globe covered with water before the six "days," or periods, of special creative works began. "There was darkness upon the surface of the watery deep." (Genesis 1:2) At that early point, something—perhaps a mixture of water vapor, other gases, and volcanic dust—must have prevented sunlight from reaching

*Creative works on "days" one through three made possible vegetation in awesome variety*

the surface of the earth. The Bible describes the first creative period this way: "God proceeded to say, 'Let there be light'; and gradually light came into existence," or reached the surface of the earth.—Genesis 1:3, translation by J. W. Watts.

The expression "gradually . . . came" accurately reflects a form of the Hebrew verb involved, denoting a progressive action that takes time to complete. Anyone who reads the Hebrew language can find this form some 40 times in Genesis chapter 1, and it is a key to understanding the chapter. What God began in the figurative evening of a creative period, or age, became progressively clear, or apparent, after the morning of that "day."* Also, what was started in one period did not have to be fully completed when the next period began. To illustrate, light gradually began to appear on the first "day," yet it was not until the

---

* The Hebrews counted their day as commencing in the evening and running until the following sunset.

fourth creative period that the sun, moon, and stars could have been discerned.—Genesis 1:14-19.

## The Second and Third "Days"

Before the Creator made dry land appear on the third creative "day," he lifted some of the waters. As a result, the earth was surrounded by a blanket of water vapor.* The ancient record does not—and need not—describe the mechanisms used. Instead, the Bible focuses on the expanse between the upper and surface waters. It calls this the heavens. Even today people use this term for the atmosphere where birds and airplanes fly. In due course, God filled this atmospheric heavens with a mix of gases vital for life.

However, during the creative "days," the surface water subsided, so that land appeared. Perhaps using geologic forces that are still moving the plates of the earth, God seems to have pushed ocean ridges up to form continents. This would produce dry land above the surface and deep ocean valleys below, which oceanographers have now mapped and are eagerly studying. (Compare Psalm 104:8, 9.) After dry ground had been formed, another marvelous development occurred. We read: "God went on to say: 'Let the earth cause grass to shoot forth, vegetation bearing seed, fruit trees yielding fruit

---

* The Creator could have employed natural processes to lift these waters and keep them aloft. These waters fell in the days of Noah. (Genesis 1:6-8; 2 Peter 2:5; 3:5, 6) This historic event left an indelible mark on the human survivors and their descendants, as anthropologists confirm. We find this event reflected in flood accounts preserved by peoples earth wide.

according to their kinds, the seed of which is in it, upon the earth.' And it came to be so."—Genesis 1:11.

As discussed in the preceding chapter ("The Handiwork—What Is Behind It?"), photosynthesis is essential for plants. A green plant cell has a number of smaller parts called chloroplasts, which obtain energy from sunlight. "These microscopic factories," explains the book *Planet Earth,* "manufacture sugars and starches . . . No human has ever designed a factory more efficient, or whose products are more in demand, than a chloroplast."

Indeed, later animal life would depend upon chloroplasts for survival. Also, without green vegetation, earth's atmosphere would be overly rich in carbon dioxide, and we would die from heat and lack of oxygen. Some specialists give astonishing explanations for the development of life dependent on photosynthesis. For example, they say that when single-celled organisms in the water began to run out of food, "a few pioneering cells finally invented a solution. They arrived at photosynthesis." But could that really be so? Photosynthesis is so complex that scientists are still attempting to unravel its secrets. Do you think that self-reproducing photosynthetic life arose inexplicably and spontaneously? Or do you find it more reasonable to believe that it exists as a result of intelligent, purposeful creation, as Genesis reports?

The appearance of new varieties of plant life may not have ended on the third creative "day." It could even have been going on into the sixth "day," when the Creator "planted a garden in Eden" and "made to grow out of the ground every tree desirable to one's sight and good for food." (Genesis 2:8, 9) And, as mentioned, the earth's atmosphere must have cleared on "day" four, so that more light from the sun and other heavenly bodies reached planet Earth.

### The Fifth and Sixth "Days"

During the fifth creative "day," the Creator proceeded to fill the oceans and the atmospheric heavens with a new form of life—"living souls"—distinct from vegetation. Interestingly, biologists speak, among other things, of the plant kingdom and the animal kingdom, and they divide these into subclassifications. The Hebrew word translated "soul" means "a breather." The Bible also says that "living souls" have blood. Therefore, we may conclude that creatures having both a respiratory system and a circulatory system—the breathing denizens of the seas and heavens—began to appear in the fifth creative period.—Genesis 1:20; 9:3, 4.

On the sixth "day," God gave more attention to the land. He created "domestic" animals and "wild" animals, these being meaningful designations when Moses penned the account. (Genesis 1:24) So it was in this sixth creative period that land mammals were formed. What, though, about humans?

The ancient record tells us that eventually the Creator chose to produce a truly unique form of life on earth. He told his heavenly Son: "Let us make man in our image, according to our likeness, and let them have in subjection the fish of the sea and the flying creatures of the heavens and the domestic animals and all the earth and every moving animal that is moving upon the earth." (Genesis 1:26) Man would therefore reflect the spiritual image of his Maker, displaying His qualities. And man would be capable of taking in huge amounts of knowledge. Thus, humans could act with an intelligence surpassing that of any animal. Also, unlike the animals, man was made with a capacity to act according to his own free will, not being controlled mainly by instinct.

In recent years, scientists have researched human genes extensively. By comparing human genetic patterns around the earth, they found clear evidence that all humans have a common ancestor, a source of the DNA of all people who have ever lived, including each of us. In 1988, *Newsweek* magazine presented those findings in a report entitled "The Search for Adam and Eve." Those studies were based on a type of mitochondrial DNA, genetic material passed on only by the female. Reports in 1995 about research on male DNA point to the same conclusion —that "there was an ancestral 'Adam,' whose genetic material on the [Y] chromosome is common to every man now on earth," as *Time* magazine put it. Whether those findings are accurate in every detail or not, they illustrate that the history we find in Genesis is highly credible, being authored by One who was on the scene at the time.

What a climax it was when God assembled some of the elements of the earth to form his first human son, whom he named Adam! (Luke 3:38) The historical account tells us that the Creator of the globe and life on it put the man he had made in a garden-like area "to cultivate it and to take care of it." (Genesis 2:15) At that time the Creator may still have

*The Bible accurately describes in simple terms the sequential appearance of life-forms on earth*

been producing new animal kinds. The Bible says: "God was forming from the ground every wild beast of the field and every flying creature of the heavens, and he began bringing them to the man to see what he would call each one; and whatever the man would call it, each living soul, that was its name." (Genesis 2:19) The Bible in no way suggests that the first man, Adam, was merely a mythical figure. On the contrary, he was a real person—a thinking, feeling human—who could find joy working in that Paradise home. Every day, he learned more about what his Creator had made and what that One was like —his qualities, his personality.

Then, after an unspecified period, God created the first woman, to be Adam's wife. Further, God added greater purpose to their lives with this meaningful assignment: "Be fruitful and become many and fill the earth and subdue it, and have in subjection the fish of the sea and the flying creatures of the heavens and every living creature that is moving upon the earth." (Genesis 1:27, 28) Nothing can change this declared purpose of the Creator, namely, that the whole earth should be turned into a paradise filled with happy humans living at peace with one another and with the animals.

The material universe, including our planet and life on it, clearly testify to God's wisdom. So he obviously could foresee the possibility that, in time, some humans might choose to act independently or rebelliously, despite his being the Creator and Life-Giver. Such rebellion could disrupt the grand work of making a global paradise. The record says that God set before Adam and Eve a simple test that would remind them of the need to be obedient. Disobedience, God said, would result in their forfeiting the life that he had given to them. It was caring on the Creator's part to alert our first ancestors to an erroneous course that would affect the happiness of the whole human race.—Genesis 2:16, 17.

By the close of the sixth "day," the Creator had done everything necessary to fulfill his purpose. He could rightly pronounce everything he had made "very good." (Genesis 1:31) At this point the Bible introduces another important time period by saying that God "proceeded to rest *on the seventh day* from all his work that he had made." (Genesis 2:2) Since the Creator "does not tire out or grow weary," why is he described as resting? (Isaiah 40:28) This indicates that he ceased performing works of physical creation; moreover, he rests in the knowledge that nothing, not even rebellion in heaven or on earth, can thwart the fulfillment of his grand purpose. God

*"As a geologist . . . I could hardly do better than follow rather closely much of the language of the first chapter of Genesis."—Wallace Pratt*

confidently pronounced a blessing upon the seventh creative "day." Hence, God's loyal intelligent creatures—humans and invisible spirit creatures—can be certain that by the end of the seventh "day," peace and happiness will reign throughout the universe.

### Can You Trust the Genesis Record?

But can you really put faith in this account of creation and the prospects it holds out? As we noted, modern genetic research is moving toward the conclusion stated in the Bible long ago. Also, some scientists have taken note of the order of events presented in Genesis. For example, noted geologist Wallace Pratt commented: "If I as a geologist were called upon to explain briefly our modern ideas of the origin of the earth and the development of life on it to a simple, pastoral people, such as the tribes to whom the Book of Genesis was addressed, I could hardly do better than follow rather closely much of the language of the first chapter of Genesis." He also observed that the order as described in Genesis for the origin of the oceans and the emergence of land, as well as for the appearance of marine life, birds, and mammals, is in essence the sequence of the principal divisions of geologic time.

Consider: How did Moses—thousands of years ago—get that order right if his source of information were not from the Creator and Designer himself?

"By faith," the Bible states, "we perceive that the universe was fashioned by the word of God, so that the visible came forth from the invisible." (Hebrews 11:3, *The New English Bible*) Many are not disposed to accept that fact, preferring to believe in chance or in some blind process that supposedly produced our universe and life.* But, as we have seen, there are many and varied reasons to believe that the universe and terrestrial life—including our life—derives from an intelligent First Cause, a Creator, God.

The Bible frankly acknowledges that "faith is not a possession of all people." (2 Thessalonians 3:2) However, faith is not credulity. Faith is based on substance. In the next chapter, we will consider additional valid and persuasive reasons why it is possible to put confidence in the Bible and in the Grand Creator, who cares for us personally.

---

* For a further study of the history of life-forms on earth, see *Life—How Did It Get Here? By Evolution or by Creation?*, published by the Watchtower Bible and Tract Society of New York, Inc.

# CHAPTER SEVEN

# What Can You Learn About the Creator From a Book?

YOU likely agree that an informative, interesting book has real worth. The Bible is such a book. In it you find gripping life stories that set forth high moral values. You also find vivid illustrations of important truths. One of its writers who was noted for wisdom said that he "sought to find the delightful words and the writing of correct words of truth." —Ecclesiastes 12:10.

The book we refer to as "The Bible" is actually a collection of 66 smaller books written over a span of more than 1,500 years. For example, between 1513 and 1473 B.C.E., Moses wrote the first five books, starting with Genesis. John, one of Jesus' apostles, was the last of the Bible writers. He wrote a history of Jesus' life (the Gospel of John) as well as shorter letters and the book of Revelation, which appears as the last book in most Bibles.

During the 1,500 years from Moses to John, some 40 individuals shared in writing the Bible. They were sincere, devout men who wanted to help others learn about our Creator. From their writings we can gain insight into God's personality and we learn how we can please him. The Bible also enables us to understand why wickedness abounds and how it will be brought to an end. Bible writers pointed forward to the time when mankind will live more directly under God's rulership, and they described some of the thrilling conditions we may then enjoy.

—Psalm 37:10, 11; Isaiah 2:2-4; 65:17-25; Revelation 21:3-5.

You likely realize that many dismiss the Bible as an ancient book of human wisdom. However, millions of people are convinced that God is its real Author, that he guided the thoughts of its writers. (2 Peter 1:20, 21) How can you determine whether what the Bible writers wrote really is from God?

Well, there are a number of converging lines of evidence that you could consider. Many individuals have done so before concluding that the Bible is more than a mere human book, that it is from a superhuman source. Let us illustrate this with just one form of evidence. In doing so, we can learn more about the Creator of our universe, the Source of human life.

## Predictions That Came True

Quite a few Bible writers recorded prophecies. Far from claiming that they personally could foretell the future, these writers gave credit to the Creator. For example, Isaiah identified God as "the One telling from the beginning the finale." (Isaiah 1:1; 42:8, 9; 46:8-11) The ability to foretell events that were to occur decades or even centuries in the future marks the God of Isaiah as unique; he is not a mere idol, like those that people past and present have adored. Prophecy gives us convincing evidence that the Bible is not of human authorship. Consider how Isaiah's book bears this out.

A comparison of the contents of Isaiah with historical data shows that the book was written about 732 B.C.E. Isaiah foretold that calamity would come upon the inhabitants of Jerusalem and Judah because they were guilty of bloodshed and idol worship. Isaiah predicted that the land would be devastated, Jerusalem and its temple destroyed, and the survivors taken captive to Babylon. But Isaiah also prophesied that God would not forget the captive nation. The book foretold that a foreign king named Cyrus would conquer Babylon and free the Jews to return to their homeland. In fact, Isaiah describes God as "the One saying of Cyrus, 'He is my shepherd, and all that I delight in he will completely carry out'; even in my saying of Jerusalem, 'She will be rebuilt,' and of the temple, 'You will have your foundation laid.'"—Isaiah 2:8; 24:1; 39:5-7; 43:14; 44:24-28; 45:1.

In Isaiah's day, the eighth century B.C.E., such predictions might have seemed unbelievable. At that point Babylon was not even a significant military power. It was subject to the real world power of the time, the Assyrian Empire. Equally strange would have been the idea that a conquered people who had been taken into a distant land as exiles could be released and reclaim their land. "Who has heard of a thing like this?" Isaiah wrote.—Isaiah 66:8.

Yet, what do we find if we move two centuries forward? The subsequent history of the ancient Jews proved that Isaiah's prophecy was fulfilled in detail. Babylon did become mighty, and it destroyed Jerusalem. The name of the Persian king (Cyrus), his subsequent conquest of Babylon, and the Jews' return are all accepted facts of history. So exactly did these prophesied details turn out that in the

19th century, critics claimed that Isaiah's book was a hoax; they in effect said: 'Isaiah may have written the first chapters, but a later writer in the time of King Cyrus made up the rest of the book so that it would appear to be a prophecy.' Someone might make such dismissive assertions, but what are the facts?

### Real Predictions?

The predictions in the book of Isaiah are not limited to events involving Cyrus and the Jewish exiles. Isaiah also foretold Babylon's final situation, and his book gave many details about a coming Messiah, or Deliverer, who would suffer and then be glorified. Can we establish whether such predictions were written long in advance and therefore were prophecies to be fulfilled?

Consider this point. Isaiah wrote about Babylon's final situation: "Babylon, the decoration of kingdoms, the beauty of the pride of the Chaldeans, must become as when God overthrew Sodom and Gomorrah. She will never be inhabited, nor will she reside for generation after generation." (Isaiah 13:19, 20; chapter 47) How did things actually work out?

The facts are that Babylon had long depended on a complex irrigation system of dams and canals between the Tigris and Euphrates rivers. It appears that about 140 B.C.E. this water system was damaged in the destructive Parthian conquest and basically collapsed. With what effect? *The Encyclopedia Americana* explains: "The soil became saturated with mineral salts, and a crust of alkali

*Centuries after the Bible had foretold it, powerful Babylon became a desolate ruin, and it remains so to our day*

formed over the surface, making agricultural use impossible." Some 200 years later, Babylon was still a populous city, but it did not remain such for much longer. (Compare 1 Peter 5:13.) By the third century C.E., the historian Dio Cassius (c.150-235 C.E.) described a visitor to Babylon as finding nothing but "mounds and stones and ruins." (LXVIII, 30) Significantly, by this time Isaiah had been dead and his complete book in circulation for centuries. And if you visited Babylon today, you would see mere ruins of that once-glorious city. Though ancient cities such as Rome, Jerusalem, and Athens have survived down to our day, Babylon is desolate, uninhabited, a ruin; it is just as Isaiah foretold. The prediction came true.

Now let us focus on Isaiah's description of the

coming Messiah. According to Isaiah 52:13, this special servant of God would eventually be 'in high station and be exalted very much.' However, the following chapter (Isaiah 53) prophesied that before his exaltation, the Messiah would undergo a surprisingly different experience. You might be amazed at the details recorded in that chapter, which is widely acknowledged to be a Messianic prophecy.

As you can read there, the Messiah would be despised by his countrymen. Certain that this would occur, Isaiah wrote as if it had already happened: "He was despised and was avoided by men." (Verse 3) This mistreatment would be totally unjustified because the Messiah would do good for the people. "Our sicknesses were what he himself carried," is how Isaiah described the Messiah's acts of healing. (Verse 4) In spite of that, the Messiah would be tried and unjustly condemned, while remaining silent before his accusers. (Verses 7, 8) He would allow himself to be handed over to be killed alongside criminals; during his execution, his body would be pierced. (Verses 5, 12) Despite dying like a criminal, he would be buried as if a rich man. (Verse 9) And Isaiah repeatedly stated that the Messiah's unjust death would have atoning power, covering the sins of other humans.—Verses 5, 8, 11, 12.

All of that came true. The histories recorded by Jesus' contemporaries—Matthew, Mark, Luke, and John—bear out that what Isaiah had foretold did in fact occur. Some of the events took place after Jesus' death, so the situation was not one he could have manipulated. (Matthew 8:16, 17; 26:67; 27:14, 39-44, 57-60; John 19:1, 34) The total fulfillment of Isaiah's Messianic prophecy has had a powerful effect on sincere Bible readers over the centuries, including some who formerly did not accept Jesus. Scholar William Urwick notes: "Many Jews, in committing to writing the reason of their conversion to Christianity, acknowledged that it was the perusal of this chapter [Isaiah 53] which had shaken their faith in their old creed and teachers."—*The Servant of Jehovah.**

Urwick made that comment in the late 1800's, when some might still have doubted whether Isaiah chapter 53 had been written centuries before Jesus' birth. However, discoveries since then have essentially removed any basis for doubt. In 1947, a Bedouin shepherd near the Dead Sea discovered an ancient scroll of the entire book of Isaiah. Experts in ancient writing dated the scroll as being from 125 to 100 B.C.E. Then in 1990, a carbon 14 analysis of the scroll gave a date of between 202 and 107 B.C.E. Yes, this famous scroll of Isaiah was already quite old when Jesus was born. What does comparing it with modern Bibles reveal?

If you visit Jerusalem, you can view fragments of the Dead Sea Scrolls. A recording by archaeologist Professor Yigael Yadin explains: "Not more than about five or six hundred years elapsed between when the actual words of Isaiah were said and this scroll was copied in the 2nd century B.C. It is an amazing thing that although the original scroll in the museum is more than 2,000 years old how close

* Compare Acts 8:26-38, where Isaiah 53:7, 8 is quoted.

*This scroll of Isaiah, copied in the second century B.C.E., was recovered from a cave near the Dead Sea. It foretold in detail events that occurred hundreds of years after it was written*

it is to the Bible we read today either in Hebrew or in the translations which were made from the original."

Clearly, this should affect our view. Of what? Well, it should put to rest any critical doubts that the book of Isaiah is nothing but prophecy after the fact. There now is scientific proof that a copy of the writings of Isaiah was made well over a hundred years before Jesus was even born and long before the desolation of Babylon. Consequently, how can there be any doubt that Isaiah's writings predicted both the final outcome for Babylon and the unjust sufferings, type of death, and treatment of the Messiah? And the historical facts eliminate any basis for disputing that Isaiah accurately predicted the Jews' captivity and their release from Babylon. Such fulfilled predictions constitute just one of many lines of evidence that the real Author of the Bible is the Creator and that the Bible is "inspired of God."—2 Timothy 3:16.

There are many other indications of divine authorship of the Bible. These include the astronomical, geologic, and medical accuracy of the Bible; the internal harmony of its books, written by scores of men over many hundreds of years; its agreement with many facts of secular history and archaeology; and its moral code that excelled codes of surrounding peoples of those times and that is still recognized as without equal. These and other lines of evidence have convinced countless diligent and honest people that the Bible is authentically a book from our Creator.*

This can also help us to draw some valid conclusions about the Creator—helping us to see his qualities. Does not his ability to look forward in time testify that he has perceptive abilities beyond what we humans have? Humans do not know what will occur in the distant future, nor can they control it. The Creator can. He can both foresee the future and arrange events so that his will is carried out. Appropriately, Isaiah describes the Creator as "the One

---

* For details about the Bible's origin, see the brochure *A Book for All People* and the book *The Bible—God's Word or Man's?*, published by the Watchtower Bible and Tract Society of New York, Inc.

telling from the beginning the finale, and from long ago the things that have not been done; the One saying, 'My own counsel will stand, and everything that is my delight I shall do.'"—Isaiah 46:10; 55:11.

### Getting to Know the Author Better

We get acquainted with another person by conversing with him and by seeing how he reacts to different circumstances. Both are possible in coming to know other humans, but what of getting to know the Creator? We cannot possibly engage in direct conversation with him. As we have established, though, he reveals much about himself in the Bible —both by what he has said and by how he has acted. Furthermore, this unique book actually invites us to cultivate a relationship with the Creator. It urges us: "Draw close to God, and he will draw close to you."—James 2:23; 4:8.

Consider a prime step: If you wanted to be someone's friend, you certainly would learn his name. Well, what is the name of the Creator, and what does his name reveal about him?

The Hebrew portion of the Bible (often called the Old Testament) provides us with the unique name of the Creator. It is represented in ancient manuscripts by four Hebrew consonants that can be transliterated YHWH or JHVH. The Creator's name appears about 7,000 times, far more often than titles such as God or Lord. For many centuries those who read the Hebrew Bible used that personal name. In time, though, many Jews developed a superstitious fear of pronouncing the divine name, and so they did not preserve its pronunciation.

"The original pronunciation was eventually lost; modern attempts at recovery are conjectural," notes a Jewish commentary on Exodus. Admittedly, we cannot be certain how Moses pronounced the divine name, which we find at Exodus 3:16 and 6:3. Yet, frankly, who today would feel obligated to try to pronounce Moses' name or Jesus' name with the precise sound and intonation used back when they walked the earth? Nonetheless, we do not shrink from referring to Moses and to Jesus by name. The point is, instead of being excessively concerned over just how an ancient people speaking another language pronounced God's name, why not use the pronunciation common in our language? For example, "Jehovah" has been used in English for 400 years, and in the English language, it is still widely accepted as the name of the Creator.

But there is something more significant than details about pronouncing the name. That is its meaning. The name in Hebrew is a causative form of the verb *ha·wah′,* meaning "to become" or "prove to be." (Genesis 27:29; Ecclesiastes 11:3) *The Oxford Companion to the Bible* offers the meaning " 'he causes' or 'will cause to be.' " Thus, we can say that the Creator's personal name literally signifies "He Causes to Become." Notice that the emphasis is not on the Creator's activity in the remote past, as some might have had in mind when using the term "First Cause." Why not?

Because the divine name is tied in with what the Creator is purposing to do. There basically are only two states of Hebrew verbs, and the one involved in the Creator's name "denotes actions . . .

as in process of development. It does not express the mere *continuance* of an action . . . but the *development* of it *from its beginning* towards its completion." (*A Short Account of the Hebrew Tenses*) Yes, by his name, Jehovah reveals himself to be active as a purposer. We thus learn that—with progressive action—he becomes the Fulfiller of promises. Many find it satisfying and reassuring to know that the Creator always brings his purposes to realization.

### His Purpose—Your Purpose

While God's name reflects purpose, many people find it hard to see real purpose in their own existence. They observe mankind stumbling from one crisis to another—wars, natural disasters, disease epidemics, poverty, and crime. Even the privileged few who somehow escape such damaging effects often admit to nagging doubts about the future and the meaning of their life.

The Bible makes this comment: "The physical world was made subject to frustration, not by its own desire, but by the will of the Creator, who in making it so, gave it a hope that it might one day be delivered . . . and made to share the glorious liberty of the children of God." (Romans 8:20, 21, *The New Testament Letters*, by J. W. C. Wand) The account in Genesis shows that at one time humans were at peace with their Creator. In response to human misconduct, God justly subjected mankind to a situation that, in a way, produced frustration. Let us see how this developed, what it shows about the Creator, and what we can anticipate for the future.

*This letter written in ancient Hebrew on a potsherd was unearthed at Lachish. God's name (see arrows) occurs twice, showing that the Creator's name was known and in general use*

According to that written history, which has in many ways proved to be verifiable, the first humans created were named Adam and Eve. The record shows that they were not left to grope about with no purpose or instructions concerning God's will. As even any loving, considerate human father would do for his progeny, the Creator gave mankind useful directions. He said to them: "Be fruitful and become many and fill the earth and subdue it, and have in subjection the fish of the sea and the flying creatures of the heavens and every living creature that is moving upon the earth."—Genesis 1:28.

Thus, the first humans had a meaningful purpose in life. It included their taking care of earth's ecology and providing the globe with a responsible population. (Compare Isaiah 11:9.) No one can justly blame the Creator for the present state of our polluted planet, as if he gave humans an excuse to exploit and ruin the globe. The word "subdue" was no license for exploitation. It implied cultivating and taking care of the planet that humans were entrusted to manage. (Genesis 2:15) Moreover, they would have a continuing future in which to realize that meaningful task. Their prospect of not dying accords with the fact that humans have a brain capacity far exceeding what can be fully utilized in a life of 70, 80, or even 100 years. The brain was meant to be used indefinitely.

Jehovah God, as the producer and director of his creation, gave humans leeway as to how they would accomplish his purpose for the earth and mankind. He was neither excessively demanding nor unduly restrictive. For example, he gave Adam what would be a zoologist's delight—the assignment to study and name the animals. After Adam observed their characteristics, he provided names, many of them being descriptive. (Genesis 2:19) This is but one example of how humans could use their talents and abilities in line with God's purpose.

You can understand that the wise Creator of the entire universe could easily stay in control of any situation on earth, even if humans chose a foolish or harmful course. The historical record informs us that God gave only one limiting command to Adam: "From every tree of the garden you may eat to satisfaction. But as for the tree of the knowledge of good and bad you must not eat from it, for in the day you eat from it you will positively die."—Genesis 2:16, 17.

That command required mankind to recognize God's right to be obeyed. Humans from Adam's time down to ours have had to accept the law of gravity and live in harmony with it; it would be foolish and harmful to do otherwise. So why should humans reject living in harmony with another law, or command, from the beneficent Creator? The Creator made clear the consequence of rejecting his law, but he gave Adam and Eve the option to obey him voluntarily. It is not difficult to

*Isaac Newton formulated the law of gravity. The Creator's laws are reasonable, and cooperating with them is for our good*

see in the account of man's early history that the Creator allows humans freedom of choice. Yet he wants his creatures to be supremely happy, which is a natural result of living in accord with the good laws he gives.

In an earlier chapter, we noted that the Creator produced intelligent creatures that cannot be seen—spirit creatures. The history of man's start reveals that one of these spirits became obsessed with the idea of usurping God's position. (Compare Ezekiel 28:13-15.) He abused the freedom of choice that God grants and enticed the first humans into what we must call an open rebellion. By a defiant act of direct disobedience—their eating from "the tree of the knowledge of good and bad"—the first couple asserted independence from God's rule. But more than that, their course revealed that they

sided with the claim that the Creator was withhold-
ing good from man. It was as if Adam and Eve were
demanding to decide for themselves what is good
and what is bad—no matter what their Maker's
evaluation was.

How unreasonable it would be for men and wom-
en to decide that they did not like the law of gravity and to act contrary to it! It was just as irratio-
nal for Adam and Eve to reject the Creator's moral
standards. Certainly humans should expect nega-
tive consequences from breaking God's basic law re-
quiring obedience, even as harmful consequences
come to one who flouts the law of gravity.

History tells us that Jehovah then took action. In
the "day" that Adam and Eve rejected the Creator's
will, they began going downhill, heading toward
their death, just as God had forewarned. (Compare
2 Peter 3:8.) This reveals another aspect of the Creator's personality. He is a God of justice, who does
not weakly ignore flagrant disobedience. He has
and upholds wise and just standards.

Consistent with his outstanding qualities, he
mercifully did not end human life immediately.
Why? It was out of concern for Adam and Eve's pos-
terity, who had not even been conceived and who
were not directly responsible for their ancestors'
sinful course. God's concern for yet-to-be conceived
life speaks to us about what the Creator is like. He
is not a ruthless judge, devoid of feeling. Instead, he
is fair, willing to give everyone an opportunity, and
he shows respect for the sanctity of human life.

This is not to say that subsequent human generations would enjoy the same delightful circumstanc-

es as the first couple. By the Creator's allowing Adam's offspring to come on the scene, "the physical world was made subject to frustration." Still, it was not utter frustration or hopelessness. Recall that Romans 8:20, 21 also said that the Creator "gave it a hope that it might one day be delivered." That is something we should want to know more about.

### Can You Find Him?

The enemy who led the first human couple into rebellion is designated in the Bible as Satan the Devil, which means "Resister" and "Slanderer." In the sentence issued to that chief instigator of rebellion, God branded him as an enemy but laid a basis for future humans to have hope. God said: "I shall put enmity between you [Satan] and the woman and between your seed and her seed. He will bruise you in the head and you will bruise him in the heel." (Genesis 3:15) Obviously, that is figurative, or illustrative, language. What does it mean when it said that some "seed" was to come?

Other parts of the Bible shed light on this intriguing verse. They show that it is tied in with Jehovah's living up to his name and 'becoming' what is needed to fulfill his purpose for humans on earth. In his doing so, he used one particular nation, and the history of his dealings with that ancient nation makes up a significant portion of the Bible. Let us consider briefly that important history. In the process, we can learn more about our Creator's qualities. Indeed, we can learn many priceless things about him by making a further examination of the book he provided for mankind, the Bible.

# CHAPTER EIGHT

# The Creator Reveals Himself —To Our Benefit!

AMID thunder and lightning, some three million people stood before a lofty mountain on the Sinai Peninsula. Clouds enveloped Mount Sinai, and the ground trembled. In such memorable circumstances, Moses led ancient Israel into a formal relationship with the Creator of heaven and earth.—Exodus, chapter 19; Isaiah 45:18.

Why, though, would the Creator of the universe reveal himself in a special way to a single nation, a comparatively minor one at that? Moses provided this insight: "It was because of Jehovah's loving you, and because of his keeping the sworn statement that he had sworn to *your forefathers*."—Deuteronomy 7:6-8.

Such a statement reveals that the Bible holds far more information for us than facts about the origin of the universe and life on earth. It has much to say about the Creator's dealings with humans—past, present, and future. The Bible is the world's most studied and most widely circulated book, so everyone who values education ought to be acquainted with its contents. Let us get an overview of what we can find in the Bible, concentrating first on the part that is often called the Old Testament. In doing so, we will also gain valuable insight into the personality of the Creator of the universe and Author of the Bible.

In Chapter 6, "An Ancient Creation Record—Can You Trust It?," we saw that the Bible's creation account contains otherwise unavailable facts about our earliest ancestors—our origins. This first Bible book contains much more. Such as?

Greek and other mythologies describe a time when gods and demigods had dealings with humans. Also, anthropologists report that around the globe there are legends about an ancient flood wiping out most of mankind. You may rightly dismiss such myths. Yet, did you know that the book of **Genesis** alone reveals to us the underlying historical facts that later were echoed in such myths and legends?—Genesis, chapters 6, 7.*

In the book of Genesis, you will also read about men and women—credible people with whom we can identify—who knew that the Creator exists and who took his will into account in their lives. We owe it to ourselves to know about such men as Abraham, Isaac, and Jacob, who were among the "forefathers" Moses mentioned. The Creator came to know Abraham and called him "my friend." (Isaiah 41:8; Genesis 18:18, 19) Why? Jehovah had observed and gained confidence in Abraham as a man of faith. (Hebrews 11:8-10, 17-19; James 2:23) Abraham's experience shows that God is approachable. His might and capacities are awesome, yet he is not merely some impersonal force or cause. He is a real person with whom humans like us can cultivate a respectful relationship—to our lasting benefit.

Jehovah promised Abraham: "By means of your

---

* The names of Bible books are in boldfaced type as an aid to identifying their contents.

seed all nations of the earth will certainly bless themselves." (Genesis 22:18) That builds on, or extends, the promise made in Adam's time about a coming "seed." (Genesis 3:15) Yes, what Jehovah told Abraham confirmed the hope that someone—the Seed—would in time appear and make a blessing available for all peoples. You will find this to be a central theme running through the Bible, underscoring that this book is not a collection of diverse human writings. And your knowing the theme of the Bible will help you to realize that God used one ancient nation—with the goal of blessing *all* nations.—Psalm 147:19, 20.

That Jehovah had this objective in dealing with Israel indicates that 'he is not partial.' (Acts 10:34; Galatians 3:14) Moreover, even while God was dealing primarily with Abraham's descendants, people of other nations were welcome to come and also serve Jehovah. (1 Kings 8:41-43) And, as we will see later, God's impartiality is such that today all of us—no matter what our national or ethnic background—are able to know and please him.

We can learn much from the history of the nation that the Creator dealt with for centuries. Let us divide its history into three parts. In considering these parts, note how Jehovah lived up to the meaning of his name, "He Causes to Become," and how his personality showed through in his dealings with real people.

### Part One—A Nation Ruled by the Creator

*Abraham's descendants became slaves in Egypt. Finally God raised up Moses, who led them to free-*

The Creator liberated an enslaved people and
used them to carry out his purpose

dom in 1513 B.C.E. When Israel became a nation,
God was its ruler. But in 1117 B.C.E., the people
sought a human king.

What developments led to Israel's being with
Moses at Mount Sinai? The Bible book of Genesis
provides the background. Earlier, when Jacob (also
named Israel) lived to the northeast of Egypt, a
famine occurred throughout the then-known world.
Concern for his family caused Jacob to seek food
from Egypt, where there was an ample supply of
grain in storage. He discovered that the food ad-
ministrator was actually his son Joseph, whom Jacob thought had died years earlier. Jacob and his
family moved to Egypt and were invited to remain
there. (Genesis 45:25–46:5; 47:5-12) However, after
Joseph's death, a new Pharaoh conscripted Jacob's
descendants into forced labor and "kept making
their life bitter with hard slavery at clay mortar
and bricks." (Exodus 1:8-14) You can read this vivid

account and much more in the second Bible book, **Exodus.**

The Israelites suffered ill-treatment for decades, and "their cry for help kept going up to the true God." Turning to Jehovah was the wise course. He was interested in Abraham's descendants and was determined to fulfill His purpose to provide a future blessing for all peoples. Jehovah 'heard Israel's groaning and took notice,' which shows us that the Creator is sympathetic toward people who are downtrodden and suffering. (Exodus 2:23-25) He selected Moses to lead the Israelites out of slavery. But when Moses and his brother, Aaron, came to ask Egypt's Pharaoh that this enslaved people be allowed to leave, he responded defiantly: "Who is Jehovah, so that I should obey his voice to send Israel away?"—Exodus 5:2.

Could you imagine the Creator of the universe shrinking from such a challenge, even if it came from the ruler of the greatest existing military power? God struck Pharaoh and the Egyptians with a series of plagues. Finally, after the tenth plague, Pharaoh agreed to release the Israelites. (Exodus 12:29-32) Thus Abraham's descendants came to know Jehovah as a real person—one who provides freedom in his due time. Yes, as his name implies, Jehovah became a fulfiller of his promises in a dramatic way. (Exodus 6:3) But both Pharaoh and the Israelites were to learn yet more concerning that name.

This occurred because Pharaoh soon changed his mind. He led his army in heated pursuit of the departing slaves, catching up with them near the Red Sea. The Israelites were trapped between the sea and the Egyptian army. Then Jehovah intervened by opening a way through the Red Sea. Pharaoh should have recognized this as a display of God's invincible power. Instead, he led his forces head-long after the Israelites—only to drown with his army when God let the sea return to its normal po-sition. The account in Exodus does not say precise-ly how God performed these feats. We can right-ly call them miracles because the deeds and their timing were beyond human control. Certainly such deeds would not be beyond the One who created both the universe and all its laws.—Exodus 14:1-31.

This event demonstrated for the Israelites—and it should highlight for us too—that Jehovah is a Savior who lives up to his name. However, we ought to discern from this account even more about God's ways. For example, he executed *jus-tice* against an oppressive nation, while he showed *loving-kindness* to his people through whom the Seed would come. In regard to the latter, what we read in Exodus is clearly much more than ancient history; it relates to God's purpose to make a bless-ing available to all.

### On to a Promised Land

After leaving Egypt, Moses and the people marched through the desert to Mount Sinai. What happened there shaped God's dealings with the nation for centuries to come. He provided laws. Of course, aeons before this the Creator had al-ready formulated the laws governing matter in

our universe, which laws are still in effect. But at
Mount Sinai he used Moses to provide national
laws. We can read both what God did and the Law
code that he provided in the book of Exodus and
the three books that follow—**Leviticus, Numbers,**
and **Deuteronomy.** Scholars believe that Moses
also wrote the book of **Job.** We will consider some
of its important contents in Chapter 10.

Even to this day, millions of people worldwide

### Miracles—Can You Believe Them?

"It is impossible to use electric light and the wireless
and to avail ourselves of modern medical and surgical
discoveries, and at the same time to believe in the New
Testament world of spirits and miracles." Those words
of the German theologian Rudolf Bultmann reflect what
many people today feel about miracles. Is that how you
feel about miracles recorded in the Bible, such as God's
dividing of the Red Sea?

*The Concise Oxford Dictionary* defines "miracle" as
"an extraordinary event attributed to some supernatural
agency." Such an extraordinary event involves an inter-
ruption in the natural order, which is why many are not
inclined to believe in miracles. However, what seems to
be a violation of a natural law may easily be explained
in the light of the other laws of nature involved.

To illustrate, *New Scientist* reported that two physicists at the University of Tokyo applied an extremely strong magnetic field to a horizontal tube partial-
ly filled with water. The water rushed to the ends of
the tube, leaving the middle section dry. The phenomenon, discovered in 1994, works because water is weakly diamagnetic, repelled by a magnet. The established
phenomenon of water moving from where a magnetic
field is very high to where it is lower has been dubbed

know of and try to follow the Ten Commandments, the central moral direction of this complete Law code. That code, though, contains many other directives that are admired for their excellence. Understandably, many regulations centered on Israelite life back then, such as rules about hygiene, sanitation, and disease. While set out initially for an ancient people, such laws reflect knowledge of scientific facts that human experts have discovered only

---

**The Moses Effect.** *New Scientist* noted: "Pushing water around is easy—if you have a big enough magnet. And if you do, then nearly anything is possible."

Of course, one could not say with absoluteness which process God used when he parted the Red Sea for the Israelites. But the Creator knows in the fullest detail all the laws of nature. He could easily control certain aspects of one law by employing another of the laws that he originated. To humans, the result could seem miraculous, especially if they did not fully grasp the laws involved.

As to miracles in the Bible, Akira Yamada, professor emeritus of Kyoto University in Japan, says: "While it is correct to say that [a miracle] cannot be understood as of now from the standpoint of the science in which one is involved (or from the status quo of science), it is wrong to conclude that it did not happen, simply on the authority of advanced modern physics or advanced modern Bibliology. Ten years from now, today's modern science will be a science of the past. The faster science progresses the greater the possibility that scientists of today will become the target of jokes, such as 'Scientists of ten years ago seriously believed such and such.'" —*Gods in the Age of Science.*

As the Creator, being able to coordinate all the laws of nature, Jehovah can use his power to work miracles.

in the last century or so. (Leviticus 13:46, 52; 15: 4-13; Numbers 19:11-20; Deuteronomy 23:12, 13) A person does well to ask, How could it be that the laws for ancient Israel reflected knowledge and wisdom far superior to what was known by contemporary nations? A reasonable answer is that those laws came from the Creator.

The laws also helped to preserve family lines and prescribed religious duties for the Israelites to follow until the Seed would appear. By agreeing to do all that God asked, they would become accountable to live by that Law. (Deuteronomy 27:26; 30:17-20) Granted, they could not keep the Law perfectly. Yet even that fact served a good purpose. A legal expert later explained that the Law 'made transgressions manifest, until the seed should arrive to whom the promise was made.' (Galatians 3:19, 24) So the Law code made them a separate people, reminded them of their need for the Seed, or Messiah, and prepared them to welcome him.

The Israelites, assembled at Mount Sinai, agreed to abide by God's Law code. They thus came under what the Bible calls a covenant, or an agreement. The covenant was between that nation and God. Despite their willingly entering this covenant, they showed themselves to be a stiff-necked people. For example, they made a golden calf as their representation of God. Their doing that was a sin because idol worship directly violated the Ten Commandments. (Exodus 20:4-6) Moreover, they complained about their provisions, rebelled against God's appointed leader (Moses),

*At Mount Sinai the ancient nation of Israel came into a covenant relationship with the Creator*

and abandoned themselves to immoral relations with foreign women who worshiped idols. But why should this interest us, living so far removed in time from Moses' day?

Again, this is not simply ancient history. Bible accounts about Israel's ungrateful actions and God's response show that he truly cares. The Bible says that the Israelites put Jehovah to the test "again and again," making him "feel hurt" and "pained." (Psalm 78:40, 41) Hence, we can be sure that the Creator *has feelings* and that he *cares* what humans do.

From our standpoint, one might think that Israel's wrongdoing would result in God's terminating his covenant and perhaps selecting another nation to fulfill his promise. Yet he did not. Instead, he exacted punishment on the flagrant wrongdoers but extended mercy toward his wayward nation as a whole. Yes, God continued *loyal* to his promise made to his faithful friend Abraham.

Before long, Israel approached Canaan, which the Bible calls the Promised Land. It was populated by powerful peoples steeped in morally degrading practices. The Creator had allowed 400 years to pass without interfering with them, but now he justly chose to turn the land over to ancient Israel. (Genesis 15:16; see also "A Jealous God—In What Sense?," pages 132-3.) In preparation Moses sent 12 spies into the land. Ten of them showed a lack of faith in Jehovah's saving power. Their report moved the people to murmur against God and con-

*Keeping the Creator's matchless laws
helped his people to enjoy the Promised Land*

spire to return to Egypt. As a result, God sentenced the people to wander in the wilderness for 40 years. —Numbers 14:1-4, 26-34.

What did that judgment accomplish? Before his death, Moses admonished the sons of Israel to remember those years during which Jehovah had humbled them. Moses told them: "You well know with your own heart that just as a man corrects his son, Jehovah your God was correcting you." (Deuteronomy 8:1-5) Despite their having acted insultingly toward him, Jehovah had sustained them, demonstrating that they were dependent on him. For example, they survived because he provided the nation with manna, an eatable substance that tasted like cakes made with honey. Clearly, they should have learned much from their wilderness experience. It should have proved the importance of obeying their *merciful* God and depending on him.—Exodus 16:13-16, 31; 34:6, 7.

After Moses' death, God commissioned Joshua to lead Israel. This valiant and loyal man brought the nation into Canaan and courageously embarked on the conquest of the land. Within a short period, Joshua defeated 31 kings and occupied most of the Promised Land. You can find this exciting history in the book of **Joshua.**

### Rule Without a Human King

Throughout the wilderness sojourn and during the early years in the Promised Land, the nation had Moses and then Joshua as leaders. The Israelites did not need a human king, for Jehovah was their Sovereign. He made provision for appointed older men to hear legal cases at the city gates. They maintained order and assisted the people spiritually. (Deuteronomy 16:18; 21:18-20) The book of **Ruth** offers a fascinating glimpse of how such older men handled a legal case based on the law found at Deuteronomy 25:7-9.

Over the years, the nation often incurred God's disfavor by disobeying him repeatedly and turning to Canaanite gods. Still, when they came to be in sore straits and called to Jehovah for help, he remembered them. He raised up judges to take the

### A Jealous God—In What Sense?

"Jehovah, whose name is Jealous, he is a jealous God." We can read that comment at Exodus 34:14, but what is its import?

The Hebrew word rendered "jealous" can mean "exacting exclusive devotion, tolerating no rivalry." In a positive sense that benefits his creatures, Jehovah is jealous respecting his name and worship. (Ezekiel 39:25) His zeal to fulfill what his name represents means that he will carry out his purpose for mankind.

Consider, for example, his judgment of the people dwelling in the land of Canaan. One scholar offers this shocking description: "The worship of Baal, Ashtoreth, and other Canaanite gods consisted in the most extravagant orgies; their temples were centers of vice. . . . Canaanites worshiped, by immoral indulgence, . . . and then, by murdering their first-born children, as a sacrifice to these same gods." Archaeologists have discovered jars containing the remains of the sacrificed children. Although God noted the error of the Canaanites in Abraham's day, he showed patience toward them for lead in freeing Israel, rescuing them from oppressive neighboring peoples. The book named **Judges** vividly presents the exploits of 12 of these courageous judges.—Judges 2:11-19; Nehemiah 9:27.

The record says: "In those days there was no king in Israel. What was right in his own eyes was what each one was accustomed to do." (Judges 21:25) The nation had the standards set out in the Law, so with the help of the older men and instruction from the priests, the people had a basis to 'do what was right in their own eyes' and be secure in this. Furthermore, the Law code provided for a tabernacle,

---

400 years, allowing them ample time to change.—Genesis 15:16.

Were the Canaanites aware of the gravity of their error? Well, they possessed the human faculty of conscience, which jurists recognize as a universal basis for morality and justice. (Romans 2:12-15) Despite that, the Canaanites persisted in their detestable child sacrifices and debased sex practices.

Jehovah in his balanced justice determined that the land needed to be cleansed. This was not genocide. Canaanites, both individuals such as Rahab and whole groups such as the Gibeonites, who voluntarily accepted God's high moral standards were spared. (Joshua 6:25; 9:3-15) Rahab became a link in the royal genealogy leading to the Messiah, and descendants of the Gibeonites were privileged to minister at Jehovah's temple. —Joshua 9:27; Ezra 8:20; Matthew 1:1, 5-16.

Consequently, when one seeks the full and clear picture based on fact, it is easier to see Jehovah as an admirable and just God, jealous in a good way that benefits his faithful creatures.

or portable temple, where sacrifices were offered. True worship was centered there and helped to unite the nation during that time.

## Part Two—Prosperity Under Kings

*While Samuel was a judge in Israel, the people demanded a human king. The first three kings—Saul, David, and Solomon—reigned 40 years each, from 1117 to 997 B.C.E. Israel reached its pinnacle of wealth and glory, and the Creator took important steps in preparing for the kingship of the coming Seed.*

As judge and prophet, Samuel cared well for Israel's spiritual welfare, but his sons were different. The people finally demanded of Samuel: "Now do appoint for us a king to judge us like all the nations." Jehovah explained to Samuel the import of their demand: "Listen to the voice of the people . . . for it is not you whom they have rejected, but it is I whom they have rejected from being king over them." Jehovah foresaw the sad consequences of this development. (1 Samuel 8:1-9) Yet, in accord with their demand, he designated as king over Israel a modest man named Saul. Despite his promising start, after becoming king, Saul showed wayward tendencies and overstepped God's commands. God's prophet announced that the kingship would be given to a man agreeable to Jehovah. This should underscore for us how much the Creator *values obedience from the heart.*—1 Samuel 15: 22, 23.

David, who was to be the next king of Israel, was the youngest son in a family of the tribe of Judah. As to this surprising choice, God told Samuel: "Mere man sees what appears to the eyes; but as for Jehovah, he sees what the heart is." (1 Samuel 16:7) Is it not encouraging that the Creator *looks at what we are inside,* not at outward appearances? Saul, though, had his own ideas. From the time that Jehovah chose David as the future king, Saul was obsessed—driven by the idea of eliminating David. Jehovah did not let that happen, and finally Saul and his sons died in battle against a warring people called the Philistines.

David ruled as king from the city of Hebron. Then he captured Jerusalem and moved his capital there. He also extended Israel's borders to the full limit of the land God had promised to give to Abraham's descendants. You can read of this period (and the history of later kings) in six historical books of the Bible.* They reveal that David's life was not free from problems. For instance, succumbing to human desire, he committed adultery with beautiful Bath-sheba and then committed other wrong deeds in order to cover his sin. As the God of justice, Jehovah could not just ignore David's error. But because of David's heartfelt repentance, God did not require that the Law's penalty be rigidly applied; still, David would have many family problems as a result of his sins.

---

* These are **1 Samuel, 2 Samuel, 1 Kings, 2 Kings, 1 Chronicles,** and **2 Chronicles.**

*You can visit the area south of Jerusalem's wall
where King David had his capital*

Through all these crises, David came to know
God as a person—someone with feelings. He wrote:
*"Jehovah is near* to all those calling upon him . . .
and their cry for help he will hear." (Psalm 145:18-
20) David's sincerity and devotion are plainly expressed in the beautiful songs he composed, which

make up about one half of the book of **Psalms.** Millions have drawn comfort and encouragement from this poetry. Consider David's closeness to God, as reflected in Psalm 139:1-4: "O Jehovah, you have searched through me, and you know me. You yourself have come to know my sitting down and my rising up. You have considered my thought from far off. . . . For there is not a word on my tongue, but, look! O Jehovah, you already know it all."

David was especially aware of God's saving power. (Psalm 20:6; 28:9; 34:7, 9; 37:39) Each time he experienced it, his trust in Jehovah grew. You can see evidence of that at Psalm 30:5; 62:8; and 103:9. Or read Psalm 51, which David composed after being reproved for sinning with Bath-sheba. How refreshing it is to know that we can readily express ourselves to the Creator, assured that he is *not arrogant* but is *humbly willing to listen!* (Psalm 18:35; 69:33; 86:1-8) David did not come to such appreciation just through experience. "I have meditated on all your activity," he wrote, "I willingly kept myself concerned with the work of your own hands." —Psalm 63:6; 143:5.

Jehovah concluded a special covenant with David for an everlasting kingdom. David probably did not understand the full import of that covenant, but from details recorded in the Bible later on, we can see that God was indicating that the promised Seed would come in David's line.—2 Samuel 7:16.

## Wise King Solomon and the Meaning of Life

David's son Solomon was renowned for his wisdom, and we can benefit from it by reading the very

practical books of **Proverbs** and **Ecclesiastes.***
(1 Kings 10:23-25) The latter book is especially
helpful to people who are searching for meaning to
their life, even as wise King Solomon did. As the
first Israelite king born into a royal family, Solomon had vast possibilities before him. He also un-
dertook majestic building projects, had foods of impressive variety on his table, and enjoyed music
and the company of outstanding companions. Yet,
he wrote: "I, even I, turned toward all the works of
mine that my hands had done and toward the hard
work that I had worked hard to accomplish, and,
look! everything was vanity." (Ecclesiastes 2:3-9,
11) To what did that point?

Solomon wrote: "The conclusion of the matter,
everything having been heard, is: Fear the true
God and keep his commandments. For this is the
whole obligation of man. For the true God himself
will bring every sort of work into the judgment in
relation to every hidden thing, as to whether it is
good or bad." (Ecclesiastes 12:13, 14) In line with
that, Solomon engaged in a seven-year project of
building a glorious temple, where people could worship God.—1 Kings, chapter 6.

For years Solomon's reign was marked by peace
and abundance. (1 Kings 4:20-25) Still, his heart
did not prove to be as complete toward Jehovah as
David's had been. Solomon took many foreign wives
and allowed them to incline his heart toward their
gods. Jehovah finally said: "I shall without fail rip

---

* He also wrote **Song of Solomon,** a love poem highlighting
the loyalty of a young woman toward a humble shepherd.

the kingdom away from off you . . . One tribe I shall give to your son, for the sake of David my servant and for the sake of Jerusalem."—1 Kings 11: 4, 11-13.

### Part Three—The Kingdom Divided

*After Solomon's death, in 997 B.C.E., ten northern tribes broke away. These formed the kingdom of Israel, which the Assyrians conquered in 740 B.C.E. The kings in Jerusalem ruled over two tribes. This kingdom, Judah, lasted until the Babylonians conquered Jerusalem in 607 B.C.E. and took the inhabitants captive. Judah lay desolate for 70 years.*

When Solomon died, his son Rehoboam came to power and made life hard for the people. This led to a revolt, and ten tribes broke away to become the kingdom of Israel. (1 Kings 12:1-4, 16-20) Over the years, this northern kingdom did not stick to the true God. The people often bowed before idols in the form of a golden calf or fell into other forms of false worship. Some of the kings were assassinated and their dynasties were overthrown by usurpers. Jehovah showed great *forbearance,* repeatedly sending prophets to warn the nation that tragedy was ahead if they continued their apostasy. The books of **Hosea** and **Amos** were written by prophets whose messages centered on this northern kingdom. Finally, in 740 B.C.E., the Assyrians brought the tragedy that God's prophets had foretold.

In the south, 19 successive kings of David's house ruled over Judah down till 607 B.C.E. Kings Asa,

Jehoshaphat, Hezekiah, and Josiah ruled as their forefather David had, and they gained Jehovah's favor. (1 Kings 15:9-11; 2 Kings 18:1-7; 22:1, 2; 2 Chronicles 17:1-6) When these kings reigned, Jehovah blessed the nation. *The Englishman's Critical and Expository Bible Cyclopædia* observes: "The grand conservative element of J[udah] was its divinely appointed temple, priesthood, written law, and recognition of the one true God Jehovah as its true theocratic king. . . . This adherence to the law . . . *produced a succession of kings* containing many wise and good monarchs . . . Hence J[udah] survived her more populous northern sister." These good kings were far outnumbered by ones who did not walk in the way of David. Still, Jehovah worked things out so that 'David his servant might continue having a lamp always before him in Jerusalem, the city that God had chosen for himself to put his name there.'—1 Kings 11:36.

## Heading for Destruction

Manasseh was one of the kings of Judah who turned away from true worship. "He made his own son pass through the fire, and he practiced magic and looked for omens and made spirit mediums and professional foretellers of events. He did on a large scale what was bad in Jehovah's eyes, to offend him." (2 Kings 21:6, 16) King Manasseh seduced his people "to do worse than the nations that Jehovah had annihilated." After repeatedly warning Manasseh and his people, the Creator declared: "I shall simply wipe Jerusalem clean just as one wipes the handleless bowl clean."—2 Chronicles 33: 9, 10; 2 Kings 21:10-13.

As a prelude, Jehovah let the Assyrians capture Manasseh and take him captive in copper fetters. (2 Chronicles 33:11) In exile Manasseh came to his senses and "kept humbling himself greatly because of the God of his forefathers." How did Jehovah react? "[God] heard his request for favor and restored him to Jerusalem to his kingship; and Manasseh came to know that Jehovah is the true God." King Manasseh and his grandson, King Josiah, both carried out needed reforms. Still, the nation did not permanently turn from wholesale moral and religious degradation.—2 Chronicles 33: 1-20; 34:1–35:25; 2 Kings, chapter 22.

Significantly, Jehovah sent zealous prophets to declare his view of what was developing.* Jeremiah related Jehovah's words: "From the day that your forefathers came forth out of the land of Egypt until this day . . . I kept sending to you all my servants the prophets, daily getting up early and sending them." But the people did not listen to God. They acted worse than their forefathers! (Jeremiah 7:25, 26) He warned them repeatedly "because he felt *compassion* for his people." They still refused to respond. So he allowed the Babylonians to destroy Jerusalem and desolate the land in 607 B.C.E. For

---

* A number of Bible books contain such inspired prophetic messages. These include **Isaiah, Jeremiah, Lamentations, Ezekiel, Joel, Micah, Habakkuk, Zephaniah.** The books of **Obadiah, Jonah,** and **Nahum** focused on surrounding nations whose dealings affected God's people.

70 years it lay abandoned.—2 Chronicles 36:15, 16; Jeremiah 25:4-11.

This brief review of God's actions should help us to recognize Jehovah's *concern* and just dealings with his nation. He did not stand back and simply wait to see what the people would do, as if he were indifferent. He actively tried to help them. You can appreciate why Isaiah said: "O Jehovah, you are our Father. . . . All of us are the work of your hand." (Isaiah 64:8) Accordingly, many today refer to the Creator as "Father," for he responds as would a *loving, interested* human father. However, he also recognizes that we must be responsible for our own course and its outcome.

After the nation experienced a 70-year period of captivity in Babylon, Jehovah God fulfilled his prophecy to restore Jerusalem. The people were liberated and allowed to return to their homeland to 'rebuild the house of Jehovah, which was in Jerusalem.' (Ezra 1:1-4; Isaiah 44:24–45:7) A number of Bible books* deal with this restoration, the rebuilding of the temple, or the events that followed. One of them, **Daniel,** is particularly interesting because it prophesied exactly when the Seed, or Messiah, would appear, and it foretold world developments in our period.

The temple was finally rebuilt, but Jerusalem was in a pitiful condition. Her walls and gates were in ruins. So God raised up men such as Nehemiah to encourage and organize the Jews. A prayer that

---

* These books of history and prophecy include **Ezra, Nehemiah, Esther, Haggai, Zechariah,** and **Malachi.**

we can read in Nehemiah chapter 9 well summarizes Jehovah's dealings with the Israelites. It shows Jehovah to be "a God of acts of forgiveness, *gracious and merciful, slow to anger and abundant in loving-kindness.*" The prayer also shows that Jehovah acts in harmony with his perfect standard of justice. Even when he has good reason to exercise his *power* to execute judgment, he is *ready to temper justice with love.* His doing this in a balanced and admirable way requires *wisdom.* Clearly, the Creator's dealings with the nation of Israel ought to draw us to him and motivate us to be interested in doing his will.

As this part of the Bible (the Old Testament) concludes, Judah, with its temple at Jerusalem, was restored but was under pagan rule. So how could God's covenant with David about a "seed" who would rule "forever" be fulfilled? (Psalm 89:3, 4; 132:11, 12) The Jews were still looking forward to the appearance of a "Messiah the Leader" who would free God's people and establish a theocratic (God-ruled) kingdom on earth. (Daniel 9:24, 25) Was that Jehovah's purpose, though? If not, how would the promised Messiah bring about deliverance? And how does that affect us today? The next chapter will consider these vital issues.

# CHAPTER NINE

# A Great Teacher Shows Us the Creator More Clearly

THE people of first-century Palestine "were in expectation." Of what? Of the "Christ," or "Messiah," foretold by God's prophets centuries before. The people were confident that the Bible was written under God's direction and that it contained foregleams of the future. One such, in the book of Daniel, pointed to the Messiah's arriving in the early part of their century.—Luke 3:15; Daniel 9:24-26.

They needed to be cautious, though, for self-made messiahs would arise. (Matthew 24:5) Jewish historian Josephus mentions some: Theudas, who led his followers to the Jordan River and claimed that its waters would be parted; a man from Egypt who led people to the Mount of Olives, asserting that Jerusalem's wall would fall at his command; and an impostor in Governor Festus' time who promised rest from troubles.—Compare Acts 5:36; 21:38.

In contrast to such deluded followers, a group who came to be called "Christians" recognized Jesus of Nazareth to be a great teacher and the true Messiah. (Acts 11:26; Mark 10:47) Jesus was no impostor messiah; he had solid credentials, as is amply confirmed in the four historical books called the Gospels.* For example, the Jews knew that the Messi-

---

* **Matthew, Mark,** and **John** were eyewitnesses. **Luke** made a scholarly study of documents and firsthand testimony. The Gospels manifest the earmarks of honest, accurate, and trustworthy records.—See *A Book for All People,* pages 16-17, published by Watchtower Bible and Tract Society of New York, Inc.

ah would be born in Bethlehem, would be in the line of David, and would perform wonderful works. Jesus fulfilled all of that, as is borne out by testimony even from opposers. Yes, Jesus met the qualifications of the Biblical Messiah.—Matthew 2:3-6; 22:41-45; John 7:31, 42.

Crowds of people who met Jesus observed his outstanding works, heard his unique words of wisdom, and recognized his foresight became convinced that he was the Messiah. Over the course of his ministry (29-33 C.E.), evidence supporting his Messiahship mounted. In fact, he proved to be more than the Messiah. A disciple acquainted with the facts concluded that "Jesus is the Christ the Son of God."*—John 20:31.

Because Jesus had such a close relationship with God, he could explain and reveal what our Creator is like. (Luke 10:22; John 1:18) Jesus testified that his closeness to his Father began in heaven, where he worked with God in bringing into being all other things, animate and inanimate.—John 3:13; 6:38; 8:23, 42; 13:3; Colossians 1:15, 16.

The Bible reports that the Son was transferred from the spirit realm and "came to be in the likeness of men." (Philippians 2:5-8) Such an event is not normal, but is it possible? Scientists confirm

---

\* The Koran says: "His name will be Christ Jesus, the son of Mary, held in honour in this world and the Hereafter." (Sura 3: 45) As a human, Jesus was Mary's son. But what father was responsible? The Koran notes: "The similitude of Jesus before God is as that of Adam." (Sura 3:59) The Holy Scriptures speak of Adam as a "son of God." (Luke 3:23, 38) Neither Adam nor Jesus had a human father; neither resulted from sexual relations with a woman. Accordingly, as Adam was a son of God, so was Jesus.

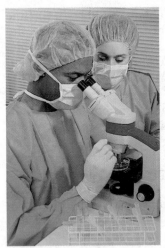

Scientists perform in vitro fertilization. The Creator transferred his Son's life to become a human

that a natural element, such as uranium, can be transformed into another; they even calculate the results when mass is transformed into energy ($E=mc^2$). So why should we doubt when the Bible says that a spirit creature was transformed so as to live as a human?

To illustrate it another way, think of what some physicians accomplish with in vitro fertilization. A life that begins in a "test tube" is transferred into a woman and is later born as a babe. In the case of Jesus, the Bible assures us that by the "power of the Most High," his life was transferred into a virgin named Mary. She was of the line of David, so Jesus could be the permanent heir of the Messianic Kingdom promised to David.—Luke 1:26-38; 3:23-38; Matthew 1:23.

On the basis of his intimate relationship with and likeness to the Creator, Jesus said: "He that has seen me has seen the Father also." (John 14:9) He also said: "Who the Father is, no one knows but the Son, and he to whom the Son is willing to reveal him." (Luke 10:22) Hence, as we learn what Jesus taught and did on earth, we can see the Creator's personality more clearly. Let us consider this, using the experiences of men and women who had deal-ings with Jesus.

## A Samaritan Woman

"This is not perhaps the Christ, is it?" wondered a Samaritan woman after conversing with Jesus for a while. (John 4:29) She even urged others from the nearby town of Sychar to meet Jesus. What was it that moved her to accept Jesus as the Messiah?

This woman met Jesus as he rested from walking all morning over dusty roads in the hills of Samar-ia. Although tired, Jesus spoke with her. Observing her keen spiritual interest, Jesus shared profound truths centering on the need to "worship the Father with spirit and truth." In time he revealed that he was really the Christ, a fact that he had not yet con-fessed in public.—John 4:3-26.

This Samaritan woman found her encounter with Jesus very meaningful. Her earlier religious activ-ities centered on worship at Mount Gerizim and were based on just the first five books of the Bible. The Jews shunned Samaritans, many of whom de-scended from a mix between the ten tribes of Israel and other peoples. How different it was with Jesus! He willingly taught this Samaritan, even though he was commissioned to go to "the lost sheep of the house of Israel." (Matthew 15:24) Here Jesus reflect-ed Jehovah's willingness to accept sincere people of all nations. (1 Kings 8:41-43) Yes, both Jesus and Je-hovah are above the narrow-minded religious hos-tility that permeates the world today. Our knowing this should draw us to the Creator and his Son.

*Many who heard Jesus and saw how he dealt with humans came to know his Father better*

There is another lesson we can draw from Jesus' willingness to teach this woman. She was then living with a man who was not her husband. (John 4: 16-19) Yet, Jesus did not let this prevent him from speaking to her. You can understand that she must have appreciated being treated with dignity. And her experience was not unique. When some Jewish leaders (Pharisees) criticized Jesus for dining with repentant sinners, he said: "Persons in health do not need a physician, but the ailing do. Go, then, and learn what this means, 'I want mercy, and not sacrifice.' For I came to call, not righteous people, but sinners." (Matthew 9:10-13) Jesus extended assistance to people groaning under the burden of their sins—their violations of God's laws or standards. How heartwarming it is to learn that God and his

Son will help those who have problems that result from their past conduct!—Matthew 11:28-30.*

Let us not overlook that on this occasion in Samaria, Jesus spoke kindly and helpfully to a woman. Why is this significant? Back then Jewish men were taught that in the street they should avoid speaking to women, even to their own wives. Jewish Rabbis did not consider women able to take in deep spiritual instruction but regarded them as "of a light mind." Some said: "Better that the words of the law should be burned than deliver[ed] to women." Jesus' disciples had grown up in such a climate; so when they returned, they "began to wonder because he was speaking with a woman." (John 4:27) This account—one of many—illustrates that Jesus was in the image of his Father, who created and assigned honor to both male and female.—Genesis 2:18.

Afterward the Samaritan woman convinced her fellow townspeople to listen to Jesus. Many examined the facts and became believers, saying: "We know that this man is for a certainty the savior of the world." (John 4:39-42) Since we are part of "the world" of mankind, Jesus is vital to our future too.

## A Fisherman's View

Now let us take a look at Jesus through the eyes of two intimate associates—Peter and then John. These common fishermen were among his first followers. (Matthew 4:13-22; John 1:35-42) The Pharisees viewed them as "men unlettered and ordinary,"

---

* Jesus' attitude matches Jehovah's, as described in Psalm 103 and at Isaiah 1:18-20.

part of the people of the land (*'am-ha·'a'rets*), who were looked down on because they were not schooled as rabbis. (Acts 4:13; John 7:49) Many such people, who were "toiling and loaded down" under the yoke of religious traditionalists, longed for spiritual enlightenment. Professor Charles Guignebert of the Sorbonne commented that "their hearts belonged wholly to Jahweh [Jehovah]." Jesus did not turn his back on those humble ones in favor of the wealthy or influential. Rather, he revealed the Father to them through his teachings and dealings. —Matthew 11:25-28.

Peter experienced Jesus' caring attitude firsthand. Soon after he joined Jesus in the ministry, Peter's mother-in-law fell sick with fever. Coming to Peter's house, Jesus took her by the hand, and the fever left! We may not know the exact process of this cure, just as physicians today cannot fully explain how some cures occur, but the fever left this woman. More important than knowing his method of healing is appreciating that by curing the sick and afflicted, Jesus evidenced his pity for them. He truly wanted to help people, and so does his Father. (Mark 1:29-31, 40-43; 6:34) From his experience with Jesus, Peter could see that the Creator values each person as worthy of care.—1 Peter 5:7.

---

You may enjoy comparing the parallel accounts of Jesus' healing Peter's mother-in-law. (Matthew 8:14-17; Mark 1:29-31; Luke 4:38, 39) Physician Luke included the medical detail that she had "a high fever." What enabled Jesus to cure her and others? Luke admitted that "Jehovah's power was there for [Jesus] to do healing."—Luke 5:17; 6:19; 9:43.

At a later time, Jesus was in the Court of the Women at Jerusalem's temple. He observed people putting contributions into the treasury chests. Rich people put in many coins. Paying keen attention, Jesus saw a poor widow drop in two coins of very little value. Jesus told Peter, John, and the others: "Truly I say to you that this poor widow dropped in more than all those dropping money into the treasury chests; for they all dropped in out of their surplus, but she, out of her want, dropped in all of what she had."—Mark 12:41-44.

You can see that Jesus looked for the good in people and that he appreciated each one's efforts. What do you think was the effect on Peter and the other apostles? Perceiving from Jesus' example what Jehovah is like, Peter later quoted a psalm: "The eyes of Jehovah are upon the righteous ones, and his ears are toward their supplication." (1 Peter 3:12; Psalm 34:15, 16) Are you not attracted to a Creator and his Son who want to find good in you and will listen to your pleas?

After some two years of association with Jesus, Peter was sure that Jesus was the Messiah. Once, Jesus asked his disciples: "Who are men saying that I am?" He got various answers. He then asked them: "You, though, who do you say I am?" Peter confidently replied: "You are the Christ." You might find strange what Jesus did next. He "strictly charged them not to tell anyone" about that. (Mark 8:27-30; 9:30; Matthew 12:16) Why would he say that? Jesus was available in their midst, so he did not want people to reach conclusions based on mere hearsay.

## The Greatest Sermon Ever

Hindu leader Mohandas Gandhi is quoted as saying that by following its teachings, "we shall have solved the problems . . . of the whole world." Noted anthropologist Ashley Montagu wrote that the modern findings about the psychological importance of love are only "a validation" of this sermon.

These men were referring to Jesus' Sermon on the Mount. Gandhi also said that "the teaching of the Sermon was meant for each and every one of us." Professor Hans Dieter Betz recently noted: "The influences exerted by the Sermon on the Mount generally far transcend the borderlines of Judaism and Christianity, or even Western culture." He added that this sermon has "a peculiarly universalistic appeal."

Why not read this relatively short but fascinating discourse? You will find it in Matthew chapters 5 to 7 and at Luke 6:20-49. Here are some highlights that we can reap from this greatest sermon:

**How to be happy**
—Matthew 5:3-12; Luke 6:20-23.

**How to maintain self-respect**
—Matthew 5:14-16, 37; 6:2-4, 16-18; Luke 6:43-45.

**How to improve relations with others**
—Matthew 5:22-26, 38-48; 7:1-5, 12; Luke 6:27-38, 41, 42.

**How to lessen marital problems**
—Matthew 5:27-32.

**How to cope with anxiety**
—Matthew 6:25-34.

**How to recognize religious fraud**
—Matthew 6:5-8, 16-18; 7:15-23.

**How to find the meaning of life**
—Matthew 6:9-13, 19-24, 33; 7:7-11, 13, 14, 24-27; Luke 6:46-49.

That is logical, is it not? (John 10:24-26) The point is, our Creator likewise wants us to find out about him through our own investigation of solid evidence. He expects us to have convictions based on facts. —Acts 17:27.

As you might imagine, some of Jesus' countrymen did not accept him, despite ample evidence that he had the Creator's support. Many, being preoccupied with their position or with political goals, did not find this sincere but humble Messiah to their liking. As his ministry drew to a close, Jesus said: "Jerusalem, the killer of the prophets and stoner of those sent forth to her,—how often I wanted to gather your children together . . . But you people did not want it. Look! Your house is abandoned to you." (Matthew 23:37, 38) This changed situation for that nation marked a significant step in the realization of God's purpose for blessing all nations.

Soon thereafter Peter and three other apostles heard Jesus give a detailed prophecy about "the conclusion of the system of things."* What Jesus foretold had an initial fulfillment during the Roman attack on and destruction of Jerusalem in 66-70 C.E. History bears out that what Jesus predicted did occur. Peter witnessed many of the very things that Jesus foretold, and this is reflected in **1** and **2 Peter,** two books that Peter wrote.—1 Peter 1:13; 4:7; 5:7, 8; 2 Peter 3:1-3, 11, 12.

During his ministry Jesus had patiently extended kindness to the Jews around him. But he did not

---

* We can read that prophecy in Matthew chapter 24, Mark chapter 13, and Luke chapter 21.

shrink from condemning wickedness. This helped Peter, and it should help us, to understand our Creator more fully. As he saw other things fulfilling Jesus' prophecy, Peter wrote that Christians should keep "close in mind the presence of the day of Jehovah." Peter also said: "Jehovah is not slow respecting his promise, as some people consider slowness, but he is patient with you because he does not desire any to be destroyed but desires all to attain to repentance." Then Peter offered words of encouragement about 'new heavens and a new earth in which righteousness will dwell.' (2 Peter 3:3-13) Do we, as did Peter, appreciate God's qualities mirrored in Jesus, and do we manifest trust in his promises for the future?

*Jesus washed the apostles' feet, setting a pattern of humility that the Creator appreciates*

### Why Did Jesus Die?

On his last night with the apostles, Jesus shared a special meal with them. At such a meal, a Jewish host would show hospitality by washing the feet of guests, who might have walked over dusty roads in sandals. No one offered to do this for Jesus, however. So he humbly rose, took a towel and a basin, and started to wash the apostles' feet. When Peter's turn came, he was ashamed to accept this service from Jesus. Peter said: "You will certainly never wash my feet." "Unless I wash you," Jesus responded, "you have no part with me." He knew that he was soon to die, so Jesus added: "If I, although Lord and Teacher, washed your feet, you also ought to wash the feet of one another. For I set the pattern for you, that, just as I did to you, you should do also."—John 13:5-17.

Decades later Peter urged Christians to imitate Jesus, not in a foot-washing ritual, but in humbly serving others rather than "lording it over" them. Peter also realized that Jesus' example proved that "God opposes the haughty ones, but he gives undeserved kindness to the humble ones." What a lesson about the Creator! (1 Peter 5:1-5; Psalm 18:35) Yet, Peter learned more.

After that final meal, Judas Iscariot, who was an apostle but became a thief, led a band of armed men to arrest Jesus. As they did so, Peter reacted. He drew a sword and wounded a man in the mob. Jesus corrected Peter: "Return your sword to its place, for all those who take the sword will perish by the sword." Then, as Peter looked on, Jesus touched the man, healing him. (Matthew 26:47-52; Luke 22:49-51) Clearly, Jesus lived up to his teaching to "continue to love your enemies" in imitation of his Father, who "makes his sun rise upon wicked people and good and makes it rain upon righteous people and unrighteous."—Matthew 5:44, 45.

During the course of that stressful night, Jesus was given a hasty hearing by the Jewish high court. He was falsely accused of blasphemy, taken to the Roman Governor, and then unjustly turned over to be executed. Jews and Romans ridiculed him.

He was brutally abused and was finally impaled. Much of that mistreatment fulfilled prophecies written centuries earlier. Even soldiers observing Jesus on the torture stake admitted: "Certainly this was God's Son."—Matthew 26:57–27:54; John 18:12–19:37.

Those developments must have caused Peter and others to ask, 'Why did the Christ have to die?' It was only later that they understood. For one thing, those events fulfilled the prophecy in Isaiah chapter 53, which showed that the Christ would make liberation available not for the Jews only but for all mankind. Peter wrote: "He himself bore our sins in his own body upon the stake, in order that we might be done with sins and live to righteousness. And 'by his stripes you were healed.'" (1 Peter 2:21-25) Peter grasped the sense of a truth that Jesus had presented: "The Son of man came, not to be ministered to, but to minister and to give his soul a ransom in exchange for many." (Matthew 20:28) Yes, Jesus had to lay down his right to life as a perfect human so as to repurchase mankind from the sinful state inherited from Adam. That is a basic Bible teaching —the ransom.

What does the ransom involve? You might think of it this way: Suppose you had a computer but one of its electronic files was corrupted by an error (or virus) that someone had planted in an otherwise perfect program. That illustrates the effect of what Adam did when he deliberately disobeyed God, or sinned. Let us continue the illustration. Whatever copies you might make of the corrupted electronic file would be affected. However, all need not be

*A computer error (or virus) can be purged from the system; mankind needs Jesus' ransom in order to be rid of inherited imperfection*

lost. With a special program, you could detect and purge the corrupting error from your files and computer. Comparably, mankind has received a "virus," sin, from Adam and Eve, and we need outside help to wipe it out. (Romans 5:12) According to the Bible, God provided for this cleansing through Jesus' death. It is a loving provision from which we can benefit.—1 Corinthians 15:22.

Appreciating what Jesus did moved Peter to "live the remainder of his time in the flesh, no more for the desires of men, but for God's will." For Peter as well as for us, this would mean avoiding corrupt habits and immoral life-styles. Others may try to make problems for the person who strives to do "God's will." Nevertheless, he will find that his life becomes richer, more meaningful. (1 Peter 4:1-3, 7-10, 15, 16) That was so with Peter, and it can be with us as we 'commend our souls, or lives, to a faithful Creator while doing good.'—1 Peter 4:19.

## A Disciple Who Recognized Love

The apostle John was another disciple who closely associated with Jesus and who, therefore, can help us understand the Creator more fully. John wrote a Gospel and also three letters (**1, 2,** and **3 John**). In one letter, he offered us this insight: "We know that the Son of God has come, and he has given us intellectual capacity that we may gain the knowledge of the true one [the Creator]. And we are in union with the true one, by means of his Son Jesus Christ. This is the true God and life everlasting."—1 John 5:20.

John's gaining knowledge of "the true one" involved employing "intellectual capacity." What did John discern about the Creator's qualities? "God is love," John wrote, "and he that remains in love remains in union with God." Why could John be sure of that? "The love is in this respect, not that we have loved God, but that he loved us and sent forth his Son" to offer the ransom sacrifice for us. (1 John 4: 10, 16) As was Peter, John also was touched by God's love shown in sending his Son to die in our behalf.

John, having been very close to him, could appreciate Jesus' emotions. An incident in Bethany, near Jerusalem, deeply impressed John. Having received a report that his friend Lazarus was very sick, Jesus traveled to Bethany. By the time that he and the apostles arrived, Lazarus had been dead at least four days. John knew that the Creator, the Source of human life, was backing Jesus. So could Jesus resurrect Lazarus? (Luke 7:11-17; 8:41, 42, 49-56) Jesus said to Lazarus' sister Martha: "Your brother will rise."—John 11:1-23.

Then John saw another of Lazarus' sisters, Mary, coming to meet Jesus. How did Jesus react? He "groaned in the spirit and became troubled." To describe Jesus' reaction, John used a Greek word (rendered "groaned" in English) that had the sense of deep emotions wrung from the heart. John could see that Jesus was "troubled," or had inward commotion, great sorrow. Jesus was not indifferent or

### Man of Action

Jesus Christ was not a passive recluse. He was a decisive man of action. He traveled "to the villages in a circuit, teaching," helping people who were "skinned and thrown about like sheep without a shepherd." (Mark 6:6; Matthew 9:36; Luke 8:1) Unlike many rich religious leaders now, Jesus did not accumulate wealth; he had "nowhere to lay down his head."—Matthew 8:20.

While Jesus focused his effort on spiritual healing and feeding, he did not ignore people's physical needs. He cured the sick, the disabled, and the demon-possessed. (Mark 1:32-34) On two occasions he fed thousands of his eager listeners because he felt pity for them. (Mark 6:35-44; 8:1-8) His motive for performing miracles was his concern for people.—Mark 1:40-42.

Jesus acted decisively as he rid the temple of greedy merchants. Those observing him recalled the words of a psalmist: "The zeal for your house will eat me up." (John 2:14-17) He did not spare his words when condemning hypocritical religious leaders. (Matthew 23:1-39) Neither did he cave in to pressure from politically important men.—Matthew 26:59-64; John 18:33-37.

You will be thrilled when reading of Jesus' dynamic ministry. Many who do so for the first time start with Mark's short yet lively account of this man of action.

aloof. He "gave way to tears." (John 11:30-37) Clearly, Jesus had deep and tender feelings, which helped John to appreciate the Creator's feelings, and it should help us similarly.

John knew that Jesus' emotions were linked to positive acts because he heard Jesus cry out: "Lazarus, come on out!" And it happened. Lazarus came to life and came out of the tomb. What joy that must have brought to his sisters and the other onlookers! Many then put faith in Jesus. His enemies could not deny that he had performed this resurrection, but when the news of it spread, they "took counsel to kill Lazarus" as well as Jesus.—John 11:43; 12:9-11.

The Bible describes Jesus as 'the exact representation of the Creator's very being.' (Hebrews 1:3) Thus, Jesus' ministry provides ample proof of his own and his Father's intense desire to undo the ravages of sickness and death. And this extends beyond the few resurrections recorded in the Bible. In fact, John was present to hear Jesus say: "The hour is coming in which all those in the memorial tombs will hear [the Son's] voice and come out." (John 5: 28, 29) Note that instead of the common word for grave, John here used a word rendered "memorial tombs." Why?

God's memory is involved. Certainly the Creator of the vast universe can remember every detail of each of our dead loved ones, including traits both inherent and acquired. (Compare Isaiah 40:26.) And it is not just that he *can* remember. Both he and his Son *want* to do so. Regarding the wonderful prospect of the resurrection, faithful Job said of God: "If an able-bodied man dies can he live again? . . . You

[Jehovah] will call, and I myself shall answer you. For the work of your hands *you will have a yearning.*" (Job 14:14, 15; Mark 1:40-42) What a wonderful Creator we have, worthy of our worship!

## Resurrected Jesus—Key to Meaningful Life

The beloved disciple John observed Jesus closely until His death. More than that, John recorded the greatest resurrection that ever took place, an event that lays a firm foundation for our having a permanent and meaningful life.

Enemies of Jesus had him executed, nailed to a stake as a common criminal. Onlookers—including religious leaders—mocked him as he suffered for hours. Despite being in agony on the stake, Jesus saw his own mother and said to her about John: "Woman, see! Your son!" By then Mary must have been a widow, and her other children were not yet disciples.* Hence, Jesus entrusted the care of his aging mother to his disciple John. This again reflected the thinking of the Creator, who encouraged caring for widows and orphans.—John 7:5; 19:12-30; Mark 15:16-39; James 1:27.

But once he was dead, how could Jesus carry out his role as the "seed" through whom "all nations of the earth will certainly bless themselves"? (Genesis 22:18) With his death, on that April afternoon in 33 C.E., Jesus laid down his life as the basis for the ransom. His sensitive Father must have been pained by the agony his innocent Son went through. Yet in this way, provision was made for the ransom

---

* At least two of them later became disciples and wrote letters of encouragement found in the Bible, **James** and **Jude.**

price needed to free mankind from the bondage to sin and death. (John 3:16; 1 John 1:7) The stage was set for a grand finale.

Because Jesus Christ plays a central role in the outworking of God's purposes, he had to come back to life. That was what occurred, and John witnessed it. Early on the third day after Jesus' death and burial, some disciples went to the tomb. It was empty. That bewildered them until Jesus appeared to various ones. Mary Magdalene reported, "I have seen the Lord!" The disciples did not accept her testimony. Later the disciples gathered in a locked room and Jesus appeared again, even conversing with them. Within days, over 500 men and women became eyewitnesses that Jesus was indeed alive. People of that time who might be skeptical could interview these credible witnesses and verify their testimony. The Christians could be certain that Jesus had been resurrected and was alive as a spirit creature like the Creator. The evidence of this was so abundant and reliable that many faced death rather than deny that Jesus had been resurrected. —John 20:1-29; Luke 24:46-48; 1 Corinthians 15: 3-8.*

The apostle John also suffered persecution for bearing testimony about Jesus' resurrection. (Revelation 1:9) But when in penal exile, he received an

---

* A ranking Roman officer heard Peter's eyewitness testimony: "You know the subject that was talked about throughout the whole of Judea . . . God raised this One up on the third day and granted him to become manifest . . . He ordered us to preach to the people and to give a thorough witness that this is the One decreed by God to be judge of the living and the dead."—Acts 2: 32; 3:15; 10:34-42.

*Eyewitnesses saw that Jesus was put into a tomb (like this one) and was raised to life on the third day*

unusual reward. Jesus gave him a series of visions that show the Creator to us more clearly and reveal what the future will bring. You will find this in the book of **Revelation,** which uses many symbolisms. Jesus Christ is here depicted as a victorious King who will soon complete the conquest of his enemies. Those enemies include death (an enemy of us all) and the corrupted spirit creature named Satan. —Revelation 6:1, 2; 12:7-9; 19:19–20:3, 13, 14.

Near the end of his apocalyptic message, John had a vision of the time when earth will become a paradise. A voice described conditions to prevail then: "God himself will be with [mankind]. And he will wipe out every tear from their eyes, and death will be no more, neither will mourning nor outcry nor pain be anymore. The former things have passed away." (Revelation 21:3, 4) In the outworking of

God's purpose, the promise that God made to Abraham will be fulfilled.—Genesis 12:3; 18:18.

Life then will be "real life," comparable to what lay before Adam when he was created. (1 Timothy 6:19) No longer will mankind grope to find their Creator and to understand their relationship with him. However, you may well ask, 'When will that come about? And why is it that our caring Creator permits evil and suffering to exist down to this time?' Let us next consider those questions.

---

### Jesus Moved Them to Act

In the book of **Acts,** we can find a historical record of how Peter, John, and others bore witness about Jesus' resurrection. A large part of the book relates events involving an intelligent student of law named Saul, or Paul, who had violently opposed Christianity. The resurrected Jesus appeared to him. (Acts 9:1-16) Having indisputable proof that Jesus was alive in heaven, Paul thereafter witnessed zealously about this fact to Jews and non-Jews, including philosophers and rulers. It is impressive to read what he said to such educated, influential men.—Acts 17:1-3, 16-34; 26:1-29.

Over some decades, Paul wrote many books of the so-called New Testament, or the Christian Greek Scriptures. Most Bibles contain a table of contents, or list of books. Paul wrote 14 of them, from **Romans** through **Hebrews.** These provided deep truths and wise guidance for Christians back then. They are even more valuable to us, who lack direct access to the apostles and other witnesses of Jesus' teachings, works, and resurrection. You will find that Paul's writings can help you in your family life, in your dealings with fellow workers and neighbors, and in your directing your life so that it has real meaning and brings you satisfaction.

# CHAPTER TEN

# If the Creator Cares, Why So Much Suffering?

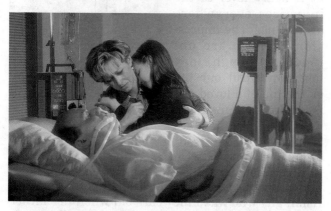

AS YOUR watch ticks off 60 seconds, more than 30 people die from infectious diseases, 11 lose the battle against cancer, and 9 are cut down by heart disease. And you know that those are just some of the diseases afflicting people; many suffer and die from other causes.

In 1996, a clock in the lobby of the United Nations building in New York City symbolically ticked for each baby born into a poor family—47 times a minute. From another perspective, every time the earth rotates, 20 percent of its population goes to bed hungry. And what if you tried to calculate the amount of crime where you live?

We must face the fact that suffering abounds in the world around us today.

"Yet," says an ex-police officer "many of us remain untouched at a heart level to the injustices everywhere around us." The impression that we are untouched, though, may last only until our life or the life of a loved one is involved. For instance, put yourself in the place

*Many believe in the cycle of Karma, from birth to death*

of Masako, who nursed her mother and her father as both suffered with cancer. While they lost weight and groaned in pain, Masako felt enwrapped in helplessness. Or think of the despair of Sharada, an Asian girl who was nine years old when her father sold her for $14 (U.S.). Taken from her village to a foreign city, she was forced to offer sexual favors to six men a day.

Why does such suffering abound? And why does the Creator not stop it? Because of such suffering, many turn their back on God. The mother of the ex-policeman mentioned above became the victim of a psychopath. He explains his reaction: "The thought of a sovereign, loving God who controlled the universe had never been farther from my mind." You too may ask, 'Why?' Yes, why does such suffering exist? What is the cause, and is the Creator concerned about it?

### Is a Previous Life Causing Suffering?

Around the globe, millions believe that the cause of suffering is a person's past; his present suffering is punishment for what he did in a past life. "Human suffering is due to our being bound in Karma, for all of us, as soon as we are born, carry a heavy burden of past Karma."* That view was offered by Daisetz T. Suzuki, a philosopher who popularized Zen in Western society. Hindu sages had devised "the law of Karma" as they groped to explain human suffering. But is their explanation of suffering reasonable or truly satisfying?

One Buddhist woman said: "I thought it did not make sense to have to suffer for something I was born with but about which I knew nothing. I had to accept it as my destiny." She found this explanation of suffering unsatisfactory. You may also. While the idea of rebirth may not be common where you live, underlying it is a teaching that can be found throughout Christendom and elsewhere —the teaching that humans have an immortal soul that survives the body. This "soul" is said to be involved in suffering—either in a present life or in an afterlife.

Such ideas are widespread, but what proof is there that they are valid? On important matters like this, is it not wiser to be guided by what our Creator says? While human ideas and strong convictions can be mistaken, we have seen that God's statements are reliable.

As we noted in the preceding chapter, the sin of our first human parents brought on the ultimate human tragedy—death. The Creator warned

---

* Karma is said to be "the influence of an individual's past actions on his future lives, or reincarnations."

Adam: "In the day you [disobey, or sin] you will positively die." (Genesis 2:17; 3:19) God said nothing about Adam's having an immortal soul; he was a human. In Biblical terms this means that he was a soul. Thus, when he died, the soul named Adam died. He was not thereafter conscious or suffering.

Our Creator does not promote or agree with teachings of Karma, rebirth cycles, or an immortal soul that may suffer in a later existence. Yet if we realize what the effects of Adam's sin are, we can better understand why suffering exists today.

---

### No Immortal Soul

The Bible teaches that each person is a human soul; when a person dies, the soul dies. Ezekiel 18:4 says: "The soul that is sinning—it itself will die." The dead are not conscious or alive anywhere. Solomon wrote: "As for the dead, they are conscious of nothing at all." (Ecclesiastes 9:5, 10) Neither the Jews nor the earliest Christians originally taught that the soul is immortal.

"The soul in the O[ld] T[estament] means not a part of man, but the whole man—man as a living being. Similarly, in the N[ew] T[estament] it signifies human life . . . The Bible does not speak of the survival of an immaterial soul."—*New Catholic Encyclopedia*.

"The idea of the immortality of the soul and faith in the resurrection of the dead . . . are two concepts on completely different planes."—*Dopo la morte: immortalità o resurrezione?* by theologian Philippe H. Menoud.

"Since man as a whole is a sinner, therefore at death he dies completely with body and soul (full death) . . . Between death and resurrection, there is a gap." —the Lutheran catechism *Evangelischer Erwachsenenkatechismus*.

## From Where Did Suffering Come?

While it is hard to comprehend the whole scope of human suffering, using the right instrument can help. Just as using binoculars helps us to see distant objects more clearly, using the Bible enables us to discern the cause of suffering.

For one thing, the Bible alerts us to the fact that "time and unforeseen occurrence" befall all humans. (Ecclesiastes 9:11) For example, Jesus referred to a news item of his day—18 people were killed when a tower fell on them. He made it clear that these victims were not worse sinners than others. (Luke 13:1-5) They suffered because they were in the wrong place at the wrong time. But the Bible goes beyond that, providing satisfying information as to the prime causes of suffering. What information?

After the first humans sinned, the divine Judge, Jehovah, ruled that they had forfeited any right to continue living. In the years until they actually died, Adam and Eve faced considerable suffering. It was suffering that they had brought upon themselves—the effects of aging and sickness, the struggle to eke out a living, and the grief of seeing their family shattered by jealousy and violence. (Genesis 3:16-19; 4:1-12) It is important to fix in mind where the blame for all that suffering primarily rested. They brought it on themselves. Even so, how can we understand why suffering continues down till our day?

Although many people would object to being considered sinners, the Bible puts the facts in proper perspective, saying: "Through one man sin entered into the world and death through sin, and thus death spread to all men because they had all sinned." (Romans 5:12) The first human couple reaped the consequences of their own harmful course, but their offspring were affected too. (Galatians 6:7) Their progeny inherited imperfection, leading to death. Some find this more understandable when they consider the scientific fact that even now children may inherit diseases or defects from their parents. This can be so with hemophilia, thalassemia (Mediterranean anemia), coronary artery disease, one type of diabetes, and even breast cancer. The children are not personally at fault, yet they may suffer as a result of what they have inherited.

Our genetic ancestors, Adam and Eve, chose to reject Jehovah's way of ruling mankind.* You know from history that humans have tried all sorts of governments in an effort to rule the earth. Some men and women involved in these efforts were well-intentioned. Yet, how do you evaluate the results of man's self-rule? Has most human suffering been relieved? Hardly. On the contrary, many policies and national wars have amplified suffering. Some 3,000

---

* Genesis 2:17 presents God's command to Adam against eating from the tree of the knowledge of good and evil. In a footnote on this, *The New Jerusalem Bible* (1985) comments on what this knowledge represented: "It is the power of deciding for himself what is good and what is evil and of acting accordingly, a claim to complete moral independence by which man refuses to recognise his status as a created being, *see* Is[aiah] 5:20. The first sin was an attack on God's sovereignty."

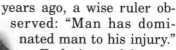

years ago, a wise ruler observed: "Man has dominated man to his injury."—Ecclesiastes 8:9.

Do you see the situation as being much different now, perhaps better? Most would answer no. Many men, women, and children suffer not only because of inherited sin and imperfection but because of what they or others have done. Think of the human mismanagement of the earth, which is often due to greed. Men are guilty, too, of causing pollution, creating poverty, and contributing to hunger or to disease epidemics. Even some natural disasters, which many call acts of God, are man-made. There is another major cause of suffering that is usually overlooked.

*Alexis, son of Czar Nicholas II and Alexandra, inherited hemophilia. We have inherited imperfection from our forefather, Adam*

## The Person Behind the Suffering

One book of the Bible is especially revealing as to what the prime cause of suffering is and why the caring Creator has permitted it. This book, Job, can clarify any blurred vision on the matter of suffering. It does so by offering insight into the invisible realm, where certain key events occurred.

Some 3,500 years ago, shortly before Moses wrote the first Bible books, the man Job lived in what is now Arabia. The record shows that Job was upright, benevolent, and well respected. He had great wealth in the form of livestock, even being called "the greatest of all the Orientals." On a personal level, Job had a fine family—a wife, seven sons, and three daughters. (Job 1:1-3; 29:7-9, 12-16) One day, a messenger rushed in to report that some of Job's valuable herds had been plundered by a raiding band. Soon another reported the loss of flocks of Job's sheep. Then the Chaldeans took away his 3,000 camels, killing all but one of the attendants. Finally came the worst news. An unusual wind devastated the house of his firstborn and killed all his children, who were gathered there. Faced with such suffering, would Job blame God? How would you have felt in his place?—Job 1:13-19.

More calamities were to come, though. Job was afflicted with a horrible disease that covered him with malignant boils.* He became so sick and repugnant that his wife blamed God. "Curse God and die!" she said. Job did not know why he was suffering, yet he would not accuse God of causing it. We read: "In all this Job did not sin with his lips." —Job 2:6-10.

Hearing of Job's vexations, three acquaintances came to him. "Where have the upright ever been effaced?" asked Eliphaz, who assumed that Job must have acted wickedly. (Job, chapters 4, 5) He accused Job of secret sins, even of denying bread to the

---

* Other passages round out the picture of Job's suffering. His flesh was covered with maggots, his skin formed crusts, and his breath was loathsome. Job was racked with pain, and his blackened skin dropped off.—Job 7:5; 19:17; 30:17, 30.

needy and having oppressed widows and orphans. (Job, chapters 15, 22) The two other sham comforters also berated Job as though he were responsible for his sufferings. Were they correct? Not at all.

The book of Job helps us to identify the root cause of Job's suffering and to see why God allowed it. Chapters 1 and 2 reveal what had recently taken place in the invisible heavens, in the spirit realm. The rebellious spirit called Satan* assembled with other spirits in God's presence. At the mention of Job's blameless course, Satan challenged: "Is it for nothing that Job has feared God? . . . For a change, thrust out your hand, please, and touch everything he has and see whether he will not curse you to your very face."—Job 1:9-12.

In other words, Satan accused God of bribing Job. This defiant spirit creature claimed that if Job was stripped of his wealth and his health, he would curse Jehovah. By extension, Satan was asserting that no human would love and be loyal to God in the face of suffering. That challenge had global and enduring impact. The issues that Satan raised had to be settled. Thus, God gave Satan freedom to act against Job, and Satan brought those various forms of suffering on the man.

Understandably, Job did not and could not know of the universal issue that was raised in the heavens. And Satan arranged things so that it appeared as if God were causing all of Job's calamities.

---

* In our earlier chapter "What Can You Learn About the Creator From a Book?" we considered the role of Satan the Devil in Adam and Eve's sin.

For example, when lightning struck Job's flocks of sheep, the surviving attendant concluded that it was "the very fire of God." Although Job did not know why these things were happening, he would not curse or reject Jehovah God.—Job 1:16, 19, 21.

If you analyze the circumstances behind Job's experience, you will see that the issue is, Will humans serve Jehovah out of love, despite troubles? Job helped to answer that. Only true love for God could have moved a person to remain faithful to Jehovah, which is what Job did. What a testimony against Satan's false accusations! This case, however, did not begin and end with Job back then; it has extended for centuries. We are involved too.

How do many react when they see or face suffering, whatever its cause? They may be unaware of the issues raised in Job's day, or they may not believe that Satan even exists. Hence, often they doubt that there is a Creator, or they blame him for the suffering. How do you feel about this? From what you know of the Creator, would you not concur with the Bible writer James? Despite suffering, he had this conviction: "When under trial, let no one say: 'I am being tried by God.' For with evil things God cannot be tried nor does he himself try anyone." —James 1:13.

We have a valuable aid in getting the wise view. That is, our considering Jesus' case. We know that Jesus is esteemed for his insight, knowledge, and ability as a teacher. Where did he stand regarding Satan and suffering? Jesus was certain that Satan the Devil both exists and can cause suffering. Satan, who tried to break Job's integrity, overtly tried to do the same to Jesus. Beyond proving that Satan is real, this shows that the challenge raised in Job's day was continuing. As did Job, Jesus proved faithful to the Creator even at the cost of riches and power and although it caused him physical suffering and death on a torture stake. Jesus' case shows that God was still allowing humans to demonstrate that they would be loyal to him despite problems.—Luke 4:1-13; 8:27-34; 11:14-22; John 19:1-30.

### Time Passes—For Good Reason

In understanding suffering, we have to recognize that accidents, sinful human tendencies, man's mismanagement of the earth, and Satan the Devil are causes for suffering. However, knowing what is behind suffering is not enough. When one is afflicted, it would be easy to feel as did the ancient prophet Habakkuk when he said: "How long, O Jehovah, must I cry for help, and you do not hear? How long

---

#### Has It Been So Long?

From Job's day to Jesus' might seem like a long time for suffering to continue—some 1,600 years. For a human, 100 years would appear a long time to wait for suffering to end. But we must recognize that the key issues that Satan raised reflected negatively on the Creator. In God's view the subsequent allowance of suffering and wickedness has been brief. He is "the King of eternity" for whom 'a thousand years are but as yesterday when it is past.' (1 Timothy 1:17; Psalm 90:4) And for humans granted permanent life, this period of history in which suffering existed will seem quite short too.

shall I call to you for aid from violence, and you do not save? Why is it that you make me see what is hurtful, and you keep looking upon mere trouble? And why are despoiling and violence in front of me, and why does quarreling occur, and why is strife carried?" (Habakkuk 1:2, 3) Yes, why does Jehovah 'keep looking upon trouble' without seeming to act? As the Almighty, he has the power and the love of justice needed to end suffering. So when will he do so?

As was mentioned earlier, when the first human couple chose total independence, the Creator was sure that some of their offspring would act differently. Jehovah wisely allowed time to pass. Why? In order to prove that rulership apart from the Creator leads only to unhappiness and, conversely, that living in harmony with the Creator is right and brings happiness.

In the meantime, God has maintained the earth as a reasonably pleasant environment. The apostle Paul reasoned: "In the past generations he permitted all the nations to go on in their ways, although, indeed, he did not leave himself without witness in that he did good, giving you rains from heaven and fruitful seasons, filling your hearts to the full with food and good cheer." (Acts 14:16, 17) Clearly, the Creator does not bring suffering, but he has permitted it so as to settle issues of the utmost importance.

### When Will Relief Come?

Actually, the fact that human suffering is on the increase shows that the time for it to end is near.

Why can that be said? The Bible reveals what happened in the invisible realm in Job's day, and it does so again regarding our day. Its last book, Revelation, focuses on a conflict that took place in the heavens. The result? Satan "was hurled down to the earth" with his demon hordes. "On this account," that Bible book continues, "be glad, you heavens and you who reside in them! Woe for the earth and for the sea, because the Devil has come down to you, having great anger, knowing he has a short period of time."—Revelation 12:7-12.

A detailed consideration of Bible prophecy points to this century as the time when that event took place. As you may know, respected historians acknowledge that there was a major turning point in history in 1914, when World War I began.* Since then, suffering and woes have increased. Jesus pointed to this same time period when his intimate disciples asked him about "the sign of [his] presence and of the conclusion of the system of things." Jesus said: "Nation will rise against nation, and kingdom against kingdom; and there will be great earthquakes, and in one place after another pestilences and food shortages; and there will be fearful sights and from heaven great signs." (Matthew 24: 3-14; Luke 21:5-19) These words, indicating great suffering, are having their full-scale fulfillment for the very first time in history.

The Bible describes these events as a prelude to

---

* For a discussion of this prophecy, see chapter 11 of the book *Knowledge That Leads to Everlasting Life,* published by the Watchtower Bible and Tract Society of New York, Inc.

a "great tribulation such as has not occurred since the world's beginning until now, no, nor will occur again." (Matthew 24:21) This will be God's decisive intervention in human affairs. He will act to end the wicked system of things, which has caused suffering for ages. But this will not mean the 'end of the world' by a nuclear holocaust that destroys mankind. God's Word assures us that there will be survivors. "A great crowd . . . out of all nations and tribes and peoples and tongues" will come out of that tribulation alive.—Revelation 7:9-15.

To get a rounded-out picture, consider what the Bible says will follow. The gardenlike home originally purposed for mankind as their dwelling will be restored. (Luke 23:43) You will see no home-

---

### Turning Point in History

"Looking back from the vantage point of the present we see clearly today that the outbreak of World War I ushered in a twentieth-century 'Time of Troubles'—in the expressive term of the British historian Arnold Toynbee—from which our civilization has by no means yet emerged."—*The Fall of the Dynasties,* Edmond Taylor.

"It is indeed the year 1914 rather than that of Hiroshima which marks the turning point in our time, for by now we can see that . . . it was the first world war that ushered in the era of confused transition in the midst of which we are floundering."—Dr. René Albrecht-Carrié, Barnard College.

"In 1914 the world lost a coherence which it has not managed to recapture since. . . . This has been a time of extraordinary disorder and violence, both across national frontiers and within them."—*The Economist.*

*Even while he has permitted suffering,
the Creator has provided many delights for humans*

less people. Isaiah wrote: " 'They will certainly build houses and have occupancy; and they will certainly plant vineyards and eat their fruitage. . . . For like the days of a tree will the days of my people be; and the work of their own hands my chosen ones will use to the full. They will not toil for nothing, nor will they bring to birth for disturbance; because they are the offspring made up of the blessed ones of Jehovah, and their descendants with them. . . . The wolf and the lamb themselves will feed as one, and the lion will eat straw just like the bull . . . They will do no harm nor cause any ruin in all my holy mountain,' Jehovah has said."—Isaiah 65:21-25.

What of suffering on a personal level? There will be no war, violence, or crime. (Psalm 46:8, 9; Proverbs 2:22; Isaiah 2:4) Man's Maker and Life-Giver will assist obedient humans in gaining and enjoying full health. (Isaiah 25:8; 33:24) There will be no more hunger, since the earth will be restored to an ecological balance and will produce abundantly. (Psalm 72:16) Indeed, sources of suffering that we now see will be things of the past.—Isaiah 14:7.

This certainly qualifies as the best of news. Yet, some might feel that there still are two dark clouds, so to speak. A person's enjoyment of those blessings would be limited if he had to expect that after just 70 or 80 years he would die. And might he not feel sad about loved ones who died before the Creator ended human suffering? What is the answer?

## Undoing the Worst Suffering

The Creator has the solution. He is the Maker of the universe and of human life here on earth. He can do what is beyond human ability or what humans are only starting to realize is possible. Consider just two examples of this.

*We have the potential to live endlessly.*

The Bible clearly holds out the prospect of receiving everlasting life from God. (John 3:16; 17:3) After studying the genes in human cells, Dr. Michael Fossel reported that the quality of male reproductive cells does not deteriorate with age. "The genes we already possess, properly expressed, can maintain our cells without aging." That harmonizes with what we saw in Chapter 4, that our brains have a capacity hardly even touched in a present life span; they seem designed to function endlessly. These, of course, are just side points, supplemental to what the Bible says directly—Jehovah will make it possible for us to live forever without suffering. Notice what he promises in the final book of the Bible: "[God] will wipe out every tear from their eyes, and death will be no more, neither will mourning nor outcry nor pain be anymore."—Revelation 21:4.

*The Creator is capable of helping someone who suffered and died—bringing him back to life, resurrecting him.*

Lazarus was one who was resurrected. (John 11:17-45; see pages 158-60.) Professor Donald MacKay used the illustration of a computer file. He wrote that the destruction of a computer does not necessarily mean the permanent end of an equation or a process that was on it. The same equation or process could be put into a new computer and run there "if the mathematician so desires." Professor MacKay continued: "Mechanistic brain science

---

### Resurrection of the Person Possible?

Neurologist Richard M. Restak commented about the human brain and its neurons. "All that we are and all that we have done could be read by an observer capable of deciphering the connections and circuits that have been established within our 50 billion nerve cells." If that is so, would not our loving Creator, with the information that he has, be able to rebuild a person?

## Your Connections Are Numbered

Jesus said: "The very hairs of your head are all numbered." (Matthew 10:29-31) What about the gray matter inside your head? Brain cells (called neurons) are so small that they can be seen only with a powerful microscope. Imagine your trying to count, not just neurons, but the smaller interconnections (synapses), which may be up to 250,000 for some neurons.

Dr. Peter Huttenlocher, using the powerful electron microscope, pioneered the counting of neuronal connections from autopsies—of fetuses, of deceased babies, and of old people. Surprisingly, all the samples, each about the size of a pinhead, had roughly the same number of neurons, some 70,000.

Then Dr. Huttenlocher began counting the number of neuronal, or brain-cell, connections *in such tiny samples.* The fetus' neurons had 124 million connections; those of a newborn had 253 million; an eight-month-old had 572 million. Dr. Huttenlocher found that thereafter as a child grew, the number gradually decreased.

These findings are of interest in view of what the Bible says about the resurrection. (John 5:28, 29) An adult has for his *entire brain* about one million billion neuronal connections, that is, 1 with 15 zeros. Does the Creator have the ability not only to count these connections but also to reconstruct them?

*The World Book Encyclopedia* gives the number of stars in the universe as 200 billion billion, or 2 with 20 zeros. The Creator knows all these stars by name. (Isaiah 40:26) Thus, it is well within his ability to recall and reconstruct the neuronal connections making up the memories and feelings of humans he chooses to resurrect.

would seem to raise equally little objection to the hope of eternal life expressed in [the Bible], with its characteristic emphasis on the 'resurrection.'" If a human died, the Creator could later bring him back to life, as he did with Jesus and as Jesus did with Lazarus. MacKay concluded that a person's death would pose no barrier to his being restored to life in a new body "if our Creator so wishes."

Yes, the ultimate solution rests with our Creator. He alone can fully remove suffering, reverse the effects of sin, and undo death. Jesus Christ told his disciples about an outstanding development that is yet ahead of us. He said: "The hour is coming in which all those in the memorial tombs will hear his voice and come out."—John 5:28, 29.

Just think of it! The Sovereign Ruler of the universe is ready and able to restore to life those in his memory. These will be given opportunity to prove themselves worthy of receiving "the real life." —1 Timothy 6:19; Acts 24:15.

Are we, though, called upon to do anything now while we await full relief from human suffering? And if so, might this make our life even more meaningful today? Let us see.

CHAPTER ELEVEN

# Add Meaning to
# Your Life Permanently

WHEREVER we live, we hear of scientific discoveries. Biologists, oceanographers, and others keep adding to man's knowledge about our globe and life on it. Searching in another direction, astronomers and physicists are learning ever more about our solar system, the stars, even distant galaxies. To what does this point?

Many clear thinkers agree with ancient King David: "The heavens are declaring the glory of God; and of the work of his hands the expanse is telling." (Psalm 19:1) Granted, some may disagree or say that they cannot be sure. But after you have considered the evidence presented in this book, can you not see ample reason to believe that a Creator exists and is behind our universe and our life?

The apostle Paul noted: "Men cannot say they do not know about God. From the beginning of the world, men could see what God is like through the things He has made. This shows His power that lasts forever. It shows that He is God." (Romans 1:20, *Holy Bible—New Life Version*) The material we covered in earlier chapters about creation made it easier to "see what God is like," to appreciate "his invisible qualities." (*New World Translation*) Still, seeing that the physical creation reflects the Creator should not be an end in itself. Why not?

Many scientists are devoted to studying the universe, but they still feel empty, finding no lasting meaning. For instance, physicist Steven Weinberg wrote: "The more the universe seems comprehensible, the more it also seems pointless." Regarding astronomer Alan Dressler's view, *Science* magazine said: "When researchers say cosmology reveals the 'mind' or 'handwriting' of God, they are ascribing to the divine what ultimately may be the lesser aspect of the universe—its physical structure." Dressler indicated that what is of greater import is the meaning of human existence. He noted: "People have given up the old belief that humanity is at the physical center of the [physical] universe, but must come back to believing that we are at the center of meaning."

Clearly, each of us should be intensely interested in what our existence means. Just admitting that the Creator, or Master Designer, exists and that we

---

### God in What Sense?

"Scientists and others sometimes use the word 'God' to mean something so abstract and unengaged that He is hardly to be distinguished from the laws of nature," commented Steven Weinberg, Nobel laureate for his work on fundamental forces. He added:

"It seems to me that if the word 'God' is to be of any use, it should be taken to mean an interested God, a creator and lawgiver who has established not only the laws of nature and the universe but also standards of good and evil, some personality that is concerned with our actions, something in short that is appropriate for us to worship. . . . This is the God that has mattered to men and women throughout history."—*Dreams of a Final Theory.*

are dependent on him may not give our lives meaning. That is particularly so because life seems short. Many have come to feel as did King Macbeth in one of William Shakespeare's plays:

> "Life's but a walking shadow, a poor player
> That struts and frets his hour upon the stage
> And then is heard no more. It is a tale
> Told by an idiot, full of sound and fury,
> Signifying nothing."—*Macbeth,* Act V, Scene V.

People around the globe can relate to those words; but when they personally face a severe crisis, they still might cry out to God for help. Elihu, a wise man of long ago, observed: "Because of the multitude of oppressions they keep calling for aid; they keep crying for help . . . And yet no one has said, 'Where is God my Grand Maker?' . . . He is the One teaching us more than the beasts of the earth, and he makes us wiser than even the flying creatures of the heavens."—Job 35:9-11.

Elihu's words underscore that we humans are not the true center of meaning. Our Grand Creator is that center, and any real meaning to our existence logically involves him and depends upon him. To find such meaning and the deep satisfaction it brings, we need to come to know the Creator and bring our lives into harmony with his will.

### Turning to the Creator

Moses did that. He realistically admitted: "In themselves the days of our years are seventy years; and if because of special mightiness they are eighty years, yet their insistence is on trouble and hurtful things." This realization did not make Moses gloomy or pessimistic; it helped him to appreciate the value of turning to our Creator. Moses prayed: "Show us just how to count our days in such a way that we may bring a heart of wisdom in. Satisfy us in the morning with your loving-kindness, that we may cry out joyfully and may rejoice during all our days. And let the pleasantness of Jehovah our God prove to be upon us." —Psalm 90:10, 12, 14, 17.

*Moses realized that however long we live, real meaning to our life involves the Creator*

*'Satisfied in the morning.' 'Rejoicing during all our days.' 'God's pleasantness on us.'* Do not such phrases suggest that one has found meaning in life —meaning that escapes people in general?

We can take a major step in that direction by sensing our place before the Creator. In a way, the growing body of knowledge about the universe may help us. David asked: "When I see your heavens, the works of your fingers, the moon and the stars that you have prepared, what is mortal man that you keep him in mind, and the son of earthling man that you take care of him?"—Psalm 8:3, 4.

And we need to move beyond acknowledging that Jehovah created the sun, moon, and stars and then caused life to abound on earth with all its infrastructure. (Nehemiah 9:6; Psalm 24:2; Isaiah 40:26; Jeremiah 10:10, 12) As we saw earlier, Jehovah's unique name indicates that he is a God of purpose and is the only one who is able to carry out his will completely.

Isaiah wrote: "He the true God, the Former of the earth and the Maker of it, He the One who firmly established it, who did not create it simply for nothing, who formed it even to be inhabited." Isaiah then quoted Jehovah's words: "I am Jehovah, and there is no one else." (Isaiah 45:18) And Paul later said of fellow Christians: "We are a product of his work and were created in union with Christ Jesus for good works." Central to those "good works" is making known "the greatly diversified wisdom of God, according to [his] eternal purpose." (Ephesians 2:10; 3:8-11) We can and logically ought to be involved with the Creator, seeking to learn his purpose and to cooperate with it.—Psalm 95:3-6.

Our recognizing that there is a loving, caring Creator should move us to action. For example, notice the link between such recognition and the way we should treat others. "He that is defrauding the lowly one has reproached his Maker, but the one showing favor to the poor one is glorifying Him." "Is it not one God that has created us? Why is it that we deal treacherously with one another?" (Proverbs 14:31; Malachi 2:10) Hence, recognizing that there is a Creator who cares should move us to show greater care for others of his creation.

We are not left on our own to accomplish this. The Creator can help us. Even though Jehovah is not now producing new earthly creations, it can be said that he is still creating in another way. He actively and productively helps humans who seek his guidance. After sinning, David asked: "Create in me even a pure heart, O God, and put within me a new spirit, a steadfast one." (Psalm 51:10; 124:8) And the Bible urges Christians to "put away the old personality" shaped by the world around them and to "put on the new personality which was created according to God's will." (Ephesians 4:22-24) Yes, Jehovah can create a new figurative heart in people, helping them to develop a personality that reflects what he is like.

These are, though, just primary steps. We need to go deeper. Paul told some educated Athenians: 'The God that made the world and all the things in it decreed the appointed times, for men to seek him, if they might grope for him and really find him, although he is not far off from each one of us.'—Acts 17:24-27.

## Meaning Springs From Knowledge

From what we have considered, it should be plain that the Creator has provided abundant information through his physical creation and through his inspired Word, the Bible. He encourages us to grow in knowledge and insight, even foretelling the time when "the earth will certainly be filled with the knowledge of Jehovah as the waters are covering the very sea."—Isaiah 11:9; 40:13, 14.

It is not the Creator's will that our ability to learn and improve be limited to a life span of 70 or 80 years. You can see this from one of Jesus' most famous statements: "God loved the world so much that he gave his only-begotten Son, in order that

*Finding lasting meaning in life opens up abounding possibilities*

everyone exercising faith in him might not be destroyed but have everlasting life."—John 3:16.

"Everlasting life." That is not a fantasy. Rather, the concept of permanence without end is consistent with what the Creator offered our original parents, Adam and Eve. It is consistent with scientific facts about the makeup and capacity of our brain. And it is consistent with what Jesus Christ taught. Mankind's having everlasting life was at the core of Jesus' message. On his final evening on earth with the apostles, he said: "This means everlasting life, their taking in knowledge of you, the only true God, and of the one whom you sent forth, Jesus Christ." —John 17:3.

As discussed in the preceding chapter, Jesus' promise of everlasting life will become a reality right here on earth for millions of people. Clearly, having this prospect can add immensely to the meaning of one's life. It involves developing a relationship with the Creator. Such a relationship right now lays the basis for gaining permanent life. Imagine the vistas that such life would open to you: learning, exploring, and experiencing—all without the limit now imposed by sickness and death. (Compare Isaiah 40:28.) What could you or would you do with such life? You yourself best know your interests, the talents you long to develop, and the answers you would seek to find. Your being able to pursue them will give even greater meaning to your life!

Paul had valid reason to anticipate the time when "creation itself also will be set free from enslavement to corruption and have the glorious freedom of the children of God." (Romans 8:21) Those achieving that freedom will have come to enjoy real meaning in life now and will have meaning in life permanently, to God's glory.—Revelation 4:11.

Jehovah's Witnesses around the globe have studied this subject. They are convinced that there is a Creator and that he cares about them and about you. They are happy to assist others to find this solidly based meaning in life. Please feel free to look into this matter with them. Doing so will add meaning to your life permanently!

# Would you welcome more information?
## Write Watch Tower at appropriate address below.

**ALASKA 99507:** 2552 East 48th Ave., Anchorage. **ALBANIA:** Kutia Postare 118, Tiranë. **ANGOLA:** Caixa Postal 6877, Luanda. **ANTIGUA:** Box 119, St. Johns, Antigua. **ARGENTINA:** Casilla de Correo 83 (Suc. 27B), 1427 Buenos Aires. **AUSTRALIA:** Box 280, Ingleburn, N.S.W. 2565. **AUSTRIA:** Postfach 67, A-1134 Vienna. **BAHAMAS:** Box N-1247, Nassau, N.P. **BARBADOS:** Fontabelle Rd., Bridgetown. **BELGIUM:** rue d'Argile-Potaardestraat 60, B-1950 Kraainem. **BELIZE:** Box 257, Belize City. **BENIN, REP. OF:** 06 B.P. 1131, Akpakpa pk3, Cotonou. **BOLIVIA:** Casilla No. 1440, La Paz. **BRAZIL:** Caixa Postal 92, 18270-970 Tatuí, SP. **BRITAIN:** The Ridgeway, London NW7 1RN. **CAMEROON:** B.P. 889, Douala. **CANADA:** Box 4100, Halton Hills (Georgetown), Ontario L7G 4Y4. **CENTRAL AFRICAN REPUBLIC:** B.P. 662, Bangui. **CHILE:** Casilla 267, Puente Alto. **COLOMBIA:** Apartado Aéreo 85058, Santa Fe de Bogotá 8, D.C. **CONGO, DEMOCRATIC REPUBLIC OF:** B.P. 634, Limete, Kinshasa. **COSTA RICA:** Apartado 10043, San José. **CÔTE D'IVOIRE (IVORY COAST), WEST AFRICA:** 06 B P 393, Abidjan 06. **CROATIA:** p.p. 417, HR-10 001 Zagreb. **CURAÇAO, NETHERLANDS ANTILLES:** P.O. Box 4708, Willemstad. **CYPRUS:** P.O. Box 33, CY-2550 Dhali. **CZECH REPUBLIC:** P.O. Box 90, 198 00 Prague 9. **DENMARK:** Stenhusvej 28, DK-4300 Holbæk. **DOMINICAN REPUBLIC:** Apartado 1742, Santo Domingo. **ECUADOR:** Casilla 09-01-1334, Guayaquil. **EL SALVADOR:** Apartado Postal 401, San Salvador. **ESTONIA:** Postkast 73, EE0090 Tallinn. **ETHIOPIA:** P.O. Box 5522, Addis Ababa. **FIJI:** Box 23, Suva. **FINLAND:** Postbox 68, FIN-01301 Vantaa 30. **FRANCE:** B.P. 625, F-27406 Louviers cedex. **GERMANY:** Niederselters, Am Steinfels, D-65618 Selters. **GHANA:** Box 760, Accra. **GREECE:** P.O. Box 112, GR-322 00 Thiva. **GUADELOUPE:** Monmain, 97180 Sainte Anne. **GUAM 96913:** 143 Jehovah St., Barrigada. **GUATEMALA:** Apartado postal 711, 01901 Guatemala. **GUYANA:** 50 Brickdam, Georgetown 16. **GUYANE FRANÇAISE (FRENCH GUIANA):** CD 2, Route du Tigre, 97300 Cayenne. **HAITI:** Post Box 185, Port-au-Prince. **HAWAII 96819:** 2055 Kam IV Rd., Honolulu. **HONDURAS:** Apartado 147, Tegucigalpa. **HONG KONG:** 4 Kent Road, Kowloon Tong. **HUNGARY:** Cserkút u. 13, H-1162 Budapest. **ICELAND:** P. O. Box 8496, IS-128 Reykjavík. **INDIA:** Post Bag 10, Lonavla, Pune Dis., Mah. 410 401. **IRELAND:** Newcastle, Greystones, Co. Wicklow. **ISRAEL:** P. O. Box 961, 61-009 Tel Aviv. **ITALY:** Via della Bufalotta 1281, I-00138 Rome RM. **JAMAICA:** Box 103, Old Harbour P.O., St. Catherine. **JAPAN:** 1271 Nakashinden, Ebina City, Kanagawa Pref., 243-0496. **KENYA:** Box 47788, Nairobi. **KOREA, REPUBLIC OF:** Box 33 Pyungtaek P. O., Kyunggido, 450-600. **LIBERIA:** P. O. Box 10-0380, 1000 Monrovia 10. **LUXEMBOURG:** B. P. 2186, L-1021 Luxembourg, G. D. **MACEDONIA, REPUBLIC OF:** P.f. 800, 91000 Skopje. **MADAGASCAR:** B. P. 511, Antananarivo 101. **MALAWI:** Box 30749, Lilongwe 3. **MALAYSIA:** Peti Surat No. 580, 75760 Melaka. **MARTINIQUE:** Cours Campeche, Morne Tartenson, 97200 Fort de France. **MAURITIUS:** Rue Baissac, Petit Verger, Pointe aux Sables. **MEXICO:** Apartado Postal 896, 06002 Mexico, D. F. **MOLDOVA, REPUBLIC OF:** Căsuţa poştală 3263, MD-2044 Chişinău. **MOZAMBIQUE:** Caixa Postal 2600, Maputo. **MYANMAR:** P.O. Box 62, Yangon. **NETHERLANDS:** Noordbargerstraat 77, NL-7812 AA Emmen. **NEW CALEDONIA:** BP 1741, 98810 Mont Dore. **NEW ZEALAND:** P.O. Box 142, Manurewa. **NICARAGUA:** Apartado 3587, Managua. **NIGERIA:** P.M.B. 1090, Benin City, Edo State. **NORWAY:** Gaupeveien 24, N-1914 Ytre Enebakk. **PAKISTAN:** P.O. Box 5214, Model Town, Lahore 54700. **PANAMA:** Apartado 6-2671, Zona 6A, El Dorado. **PAPUA NEW GUINEA:** Box 636, Boroko, NCD 111. **PARAGUAY:** Casilla de Correo 482, 1209 Asunción. **PERU:** Apartado 18-1055, Lima 18. **PHILIPPINES, REPUBLIC OF:** P. O. Box 2044, 1060 Manila. **POLAND:** Skr. Poczt. 13, PL-05-830 Nadarzyn. **PORTUGAL:** Apartado 91, P-2766 Estoril Codex. **PUERTO RICO 00970:** P.O. Box 3980, Guaynabo. **ROMANIA:** Căsuţa poştală nr. 38, P.T.T.R. Bucureşti 4. **RUSSIA:** Srednyaya 6, Solnechnoye, 189649 St. Petersburg. **SAMOA:** P. O. Box 673, Apia. **SENEGAL:** B.P. 3107. Dakar. **SIERRA LEONE, WEST AFRICA:** P. O. Box 136, Freetown. **SLOVAKIA:** P.O. Box 17, 810 00 Bratislava 1. **SLOVENIA:** Poljanska cesta 77 A, p.p. 2019, SI-1001 Ljubljana. **SOLOMON ISLANDS:** P.O. Box 166, Honiara. **SOUTH AFRICA:** Private Bag X2067, Krugersdorp, 1740. **SPAIN:** Apartado postal 132, 28850 Torrejón de Ardoz (Madrid). **SRI LANKA, REP. OF:** 711 Station Road, Wattala 11300. **SURINAME:** P.O. Box 2914, Paramaribo. **SWEDEN:** Box 5, SE-732 21 Arboga. **SWITZERLAND:** P.O. Box 225, CH-3602 Thun. **TAHITI:** B.P. 7715, 98719 Taravao. **TAIWAN:** No. 3-12, 10 Lin, Shetze, Hsinwu, Taoyuan, 327. **THAILAND:** 69/1 Soi Phasuk, Sukhumwit Rd., Soi 2, Bangkok 10110. **TOGO:** B.P. 4460, Lome. **TRINIDAD AND TOBAGO, REP. OF:** Lower Rapsey Street & Laxmi Lane, Curepe. **UKRAINE:** P.O. Box 246, 290000 Lviv. **UNITED STATES OF AMERICA:** 25 Columbia Heights, Brooklyn, NY 11201-2483. **URUGUAY:** Francisco Bauzá 3372, Casilla de Correo 16006, 11600 Montevideo. **VENEZUELA:** Apartado 20.364, Caracas, DF 1020A. **YUGOSLAVIA, F.R.:** p. fah 173, YU-11080 Beograd. **ZAMBIA:** Box 33459, Lusaka 10101. **ZIMBABWE:** P. Bag A-6113, Avondale.